WHAT GOD HAS JOINED TOGETHER

WHAT
GOD HAS
JOINED
TOGETHER

TRAVIS AGNEW

WHAT GOD HAS JOINED TOGETHER

ISBN-13: 978-1725184138

ISBN-10: 1725184133

To Amanda,

You are altogether beautiful, my love;
there is no flaw in you
(Song of Solomon 4:7).

Table of Contents

Preface

Apart from salvation, marriage is the greatest thing in the world. It is simply one of God's most fantastic ideas. No wonder Satan's first appearance is right after God institutes marriage. There is power in marriage, and Satan knows that since he has attacked every subsequent marriage throughout history.

Without a doubt, there are far superior resources on marriage out there than the volume that you are currently holding in your hands. I don't have any personal wisdom that is going to fill some void in the Christian literary world, but as a pastor, I make weekly attempts to help couples repair their marriages. In my experience, I saw the need for a more accessible and detailed book for couples who don't have the time or willingness to read a robust volume of marital concepts.

I wrote this book for those who were ready for a definite action plan to improve their marriage in specific areas. Years ago, I had the idea for a resource like this one. The thought was to call the book, *What God Has Joined Together*, and each section would succinctly address one particular item that could separate a marriage. Someone could read the book as a whole or study a standalone chapter highlighting a specific separator. I loved the idea so much that I led marriage conferences around the concept, and I even tried to convince someone else to write the book. Eventually, I could see my burden for the resource was the apparent catalyst for me to work on it personally.

I realized that while there may be better books on marriage out there, there isn't a better book on marriage written by me. As a pastor, blogger, and friend, I realized that some people wouldn't read just any book on marriage, but they might read a book on marriage that I wrote. Not because I'm anything special, but because I believe that God grants each of us a level of credibility that resonates in a certain number of hearts and minds during our lifetimes, and I wanted to leverage that precious opportunity for their good. If some people might pick up a book on marriage that could help them only because I wrote it, I wanted to be a good steward of that trust.

Laying out thirty-one possible marriage separators, I decided to keep each chapter precisely three pages in length with three simple reflections at the end of each section. Since we live in a time when we are accustomed to receiving information in bite-size social media helpings, I wanted a format that was conducive for a substantial amount of people. That type of short form doesn't leave much room for filler material, so I get to the precise point as quickly as possible. After each chapter's content, there is a scriptural passage to read, a question upon which to reflect, and a step to which you can respond.

Since the book is thirty-one chapters, one way to read it is by dissecting one section as an individual or as a couple per day. You could take a month to focus on improving your marriage. The small chapters may cause you to read more in succession – that's fine as well. One chapter's concept might be such a deep-seeded issue that you might find it necessary to slow down and unpack the implications of how to apply it for weeks. Your marriage might benefit more from stopping and working through a chapter than just hurrying on to the next one. My prayer is that this resource will help your relationship, no matter what state it is currently in, to be better by the time you complete it.

Whenever you finish a book, you look back and think fondly of all the people who helped along the way. Whether it was those people who listened to ideas or those who helped craft the work, I am so incredibly thankful. Amanda, thank you for marrying me. I don't want to follow Jesus beside anyone other than you. To my kiddos, I desire that your parents' marriage will raise a standard in your soul by which you refuse to settle underneath. Daniel Gibson, thank you for using your eager and detailed creativity to design and format this book. Ruth McWhite, thank you for offering your wisdom and insight into the editing process. To all you readers, I pray this resource further equips your marriage!

What God has joined together...

I
Let Nothing Separate

When an eternal God puts something together, it should last forever.

Since marriage is something that God ordained, it should not be cast aside as some temporary or conditional agreement. His involvement into such a pairing assumes divine adhesiveness. It only makes sense because the Bible uses the illustration of marriage to portray Christ's own unending, covenantal love for the Church (Eph. 5:25). Out of all the symbolism he could have employed to express his endearment for his people, he chose marriage.

Unfortunately, marital commitments are trivialized in our culture today. As soon as one's spouse becomes a frustrating annoyance or a disagreeable antagonist, the supposed enduring covenant becomes a contingent commitment with which to discard easily. So many marriages end because one or both parties "fell out of love." Honestly, they missed the nature of love. Anything you can fall into can be climbed out of later. Love isn't a feeling; it's a commitment.

Jesus was never married, but he created marriage. Everything was created by him and for him (Col. 1:16). So, we should pay attention when he spoke on the issue. Since he instituted marriage, he has the authority to point people to the instruction manual regarding the masterpiece he created.

One of Jesus' most unambiguous teachings on marriage involved a question asked by his adversaries, a group of jealous religious leaders who were continually opposing him. These Pharisees were always seeking a way to expose Jesus and trap him with his own words. They once asked him when it was lawful to divorce a spouse.

In his response, Jesus taught that God created people as either distinctly male or distinctly female, and God's definition of marriage from the very beginning centered on the covenantal love between one man and one woman for a lifetime (Matt. 19:4-5). God made marriage, he defined marriage, and he established marriage. Due to God's critical involvement, Jesus made it abundantly clear:

> **"What therefore God has joined together,
> let not man separate" (Matthew 19:6).**

His opponents replied: "Why then did Moses command one to give a certificate of divorce and to send her away?"

He said to them, "Because of your hardness of heart Moses allowed you to divorce your wives, but from the beginning it was not so" (Matt. 19:7-8).

Divorce was never a good option. A God-ordained covenant represented within marriage was meant to endure. Due to the stubborn nature of the people, Moses provided a legal manner for divorce to protect the families from a more profound calamity. Without a civil approach to ending marital unions, men in that culture would abandon or abuse one's disrespected spouse or merely append an additional wife or mistress to make up for the frustrating one with which he was stuck.

While divorce was permitted, it was not promoted.

Even while divorce was allowed for adultery (Matt. 19:9) or due to abandonment from an unbelieving spouse (1 Cor. 7:15), it was never mandated. God called on Hosea to buy back his prostitute of a wife as a living example of God's commitment of his love for his people (Hos. 1:2; 3:1). Why should a marriage attempt to work it out after such unthinkable unfaithfulness? Because God loves us with that type of unrivaled guarantee, and because he put our marriages together, he desires our union to reflect that type of unwavering commitment as well. I don't know how healthy your marriage is right now. I am unaware regarding the level of dedication you or your spouse have to make it work, but I do know this:

Jesus is for your marriage.

Out of all the helpful experts I could bring to a situation, no one can rival his ability to strengthen what is weak or resurrect what is thought to be dead. Even if an unthinkable sin has been committed, unimaginable grace is available (James 4:6). Despite what might seem to be insurmountable odds, we serve a completely capable God (Jer. 32:27).

God can even work in your marriage. While each situation is different, all unions could improve. If your marriage isn't perfect, then make an effort to strengthen it. If you have severely broken your vows, healing can happen, but it will take time and effort. If you feel endangered in your marriage right now, leave the premises without abandoning the person. You can work on your relationship from afar until it is safe to do otherwise. Regardless of your situation, there is hope for your marriage yet.

Different sinful ways seek to sabotage our marriages. You could probably even insert specific words into Jesus' response and see how individual dangers wrought by husbands and wives could separate a marriage. The following chapters intend to highlight different dangers succinctly and precisely in a way to equip you to combat each unique challenge.

As a son, husband, father, pastor, counselor, and friend, I've been around marriage and divorce all of my life. The following content is not dependent upon my experience or expertise. I have attempted to acknowledge dangerous areas and utilize biblical principles to address them. I have heard too often that people can't instruct others regarding marriage until they have weathered numerous decades of practice, but what that implies is that wisdom only comes through experience. If experience is the only teacher for marital bliss, then all marriages are doomed to fail.

I simply refuse to believe that. God wouldn't establish marriage to watch it deteriorate. He doesn't require an elite level of proficiency. Scripture instructs us for every single good work (2 Tim. 3:16-17), and I believe that God is including marriage as one of those good works. Within Scripture, God has provided eternal wisdom rather than lessons based on temporal experiences. You can strengthen your marriage right now with the power of God's Word. God is strong enough to keep you two together - will you partner with him?

What God has joined together, let nothing separate.

1 - Let Nothing Separate

READ: Matthew 19:1-9

REFLECT: What are the three greatest dangers threatening to separate your marriage right now?

RESPOND: What are you willing to do to combat them?

2
Let No Misalignment Separate

If you still want to be with your spouse at the end of your life, you must be heading in the same direction now.

So many marriages struggle due to misalignment. The two partners simply pointed themselves in different directions. In reality, the danger is in the subtlety of it all. Rarely do people marry another who has an entirely opposing worldview. So, why does it often feel that way in marriage? What causes a couple to get so far off track from one another so quickly?

It started way back at the beginning of the relationship. Instead of possessing opposing directions, they merely had different orientations by seemingly insignificant degrees. The compatibility of the two worked in the beginning because it appeared as if they shared similar values. They were side by side but slightly misaligned. If you looked carefully, you would have noticed that they were off by the slightest of infractions. They just differed a few degrees from one another.

Consider two arrows side by side yet slightly tilted away from one another. At first, the difference is barely noticeable. Over the years though, the widening gap is almost too immense to reconcile. As the marriage mileage increased, their distance from one another endangered their relationship which all started with a minimal difference they failed to address.

For a marriage to succeed,
a couple must possess mutual motivation.

Determine what the mutual motivation for your marriage to succeed is. You must agree upon what the desired result of the union should look like for the commitment to endure. What is the common goal for the marriage? What is the win for the home?

If you look at the pages of Scripture, a worthy goal is not to get along peacefully, raise children to be respectable members of society, or to purchase that pristine home in the country. The target must unashamedly be the glory of God. When a couple desires God to be pleased with all the aspects of their home, that mutual motivation settles most issues that arise within the marriage. Whatever you do in your home should be done for the glory of God (1 Cor. 10:31).

Notice that this marriage direction is not heading towards one another. If you focus solely on your spouse and not how to glorify God with your spouse, you will end up in a wrong direction. And while bringing glory to God is ultimately a service of devotion to him, it is also a tremendous benefit to your spouse. Seeking first his kingdom and his righteousness ensures that he will add everything needed to you (Matt. 6:33) and that you will bless your family with your integrity (Ps. 128:3).

The worst thing you can do in marriage is to make it all about you or all about your spouse. You must learn that obeying God's commands rather than adhering to your spouse's wishes is actually in the best interest of the marriage. Aligning yourself with God's standards is for God's glory and your marriage's good.

When the Apostle Paul wrote to the Corinthian church, things had gotten out of control on many levels. They had committed so much sexual immorality that some wondered if they should scrap the concept of marriage and sexual activity altogether (1 Cor. 7:1). Speaking as a single man, Paul defended marriage by citing the need to meet another's needs in practical ways for spiritual purposes.

In the hostile times in which he lived, many Christians were endangered as they lived for Kingdom causes. The addition of a spouse or children would just further complicate the decisions of a person who was almost assuredly promised persecution and, in some cases, martyrdom. Paul was single and could serve Jesus at a different pace than others who had added marital responsibilities to their missional expectations (1 Cor. 7:33-34). If lust would overcome a person, it was better for him or her to marry and have those good desires met in a healthy way (1 Cor. 7:9). If someone could live in such a way that he or she viewed singleness as a gift from God, Paul urged that person to remain in that current unattached state (1 Cor. 7:7).

His argument was simple: marry if it can cause you to serve Jesus better. If a marriage doesn't help you pursue Kingdom purposes, then stay single. Marriage is about Jesus. To embrace marriage means that your devotion to the Kingdom of God will benefit from the alignment your spouse will provide.

I say this for your own benefit, not to lay any restraint upon you, but to promote good order and to secure your undivided devotion to the Lord (1 Cor. 7:35).

Any goal less than that is insufficient in marriage. If singleness allows for undivided devotion to the Lord, stay single. If marriage provides undivided devotion to the Lord, get married.

Your marriage requires alignment. If you make marriage about your temporal happiness, you each will go in different directions. If you make it about each other primarily, you will pass by each other in the process. If you make it about worldly pursuits, don't expect heavenly benefits.

The goal of marriage is to secure undivided devotion to the Lord.

Maybe your marriage is struggling because you are trying to do it by your wisdom. Your spouse's ideas don't always align with your efforts. The standard inside you disagrees with the standard inside your spouse, and your marriage can chart a course in significantly different directions. The standard inside you is unstable, the standard beside you is unsure, so you both most look towards the standard above you. You must align your marriage around God's Word.

So, who is going to lose? Hopefully, both of you. Whoever loses his life for Jesus' sake finds it along the way (Luke 9:24).

What God has joined together, let no misalignment separate.

2 - Let No Misalignment Separate

READ: 1 Corinthians 7:25-35

REFLECT: Is your marriage heading in the right direction? Are you both pointing to the same goal?

RESPOND: In what areas do you need to align your marriage to God's Word better?

3
Let No Selfishness Separate

Marriage would be easy if your spouse weren't involved.

And he or she probably thinks the same thing about you. In reality, marriage is straightforward, but when you introduce the human dynamic, things always get challenging in a hurry.

Marriage is simple in theory but difficult in application.

The theory of marriage is simple: don't make it about you. The moment that you make marriage about what you get out of it, you set yourself up for unmet expectations which can quickly lead to justifying the absence of your efforts to meet your spouse's needs. If you could stop being selfish, your marriage would immediately become a whole lot simpler.

Selfishness blinds me to the needs of my spouse. It causes resentment to build up when my expectations are unmet. I justify what I say and what I do because my feelings take priority. I elevate my opinions to the status of truth. I can get emotional about our decisions when I prioritize my preferences regarding agendas, careers, finances, families, and hobbies.

What is the secret of marriage? Stop being selfish. Do you now see why marriage is easy in theory but complicated in the application? You married a sinful person, and so did your spouse. You married a selfish person, and so did your spouse. You married a needy person, and so did your spouse.

After graduating from college, my next few summers were filled with numerous weddings where I was an officiant, groomsman, or attendee. In some instances, we would have one couple return from their honeymoon to be part of a friend's bridal party the very next weekend. As each couple disembarked from their honeymoon and began married adulthood, you never knew what fresh piece of advice you would hear from the friend who had recently married.

On one such occasion, I remembered a friend gathering the unmarried guys together to share something he learned on his honeymoon. While I braced for the unknown, he simply stated to us, "I never truly realized how selfish I was until I got married." Within a few weeks of being a husband, he realized how out of sorts he could get when things didn't completely go his way. He's not alone. Somehow we take something like marriage which is intended to bring glory to God and to provide love for one's spouse, and we make it all about what we get out of it.

The epitome of a godly marriage is when two people decide to put the other's needs ahead of their own. Both sets of needs are real. Since both are needy people, the demands must be addressed, but what would happen if they each prioritized meeting the other's needs rather than focusing upon their own?

> *Do nothing from selfishness or empty conceit, but with humility of mind regard one another as more important than yourselves; do not merely look out for your own personal interests, but also for the interests of others (Phil. 2:3-4).*

If you could put these verses into application, most of your marital issues would begin to resolve themselves. Being self-centered is so dangerous because it can impact the marriage emotionally, physically, sexually, and spiritually. Selfishness can rear its ugly head in every room of the house and dampen every activity within the relationship.

Every single one of your marital disagreements is because one or both of you are behaving selfishly.

Test that claim. I guarantee you cannot discover one issue you have that selfishness does not exasperate. When I see my needs as more important than the needs of my spouse, my marriage cannot thrive. The only way my marriage can improve is if I deliberately renew my mind. I must show preferential intentionality to my spouse's needs. More than just lip service, I must change my way of thinking and living. My spouse's needs must become more significant than my needs in theory and practice. Only when I prioritize the needs of my spouse over my own can I truly experience a Christ-exalting marriage.

Your marriage has two sets of needs that need to be met every day. If not handled carefully, both of you will lose out. But if two needy people decide to make it about the other person each and every morning, by the end of the day, both parties' needs have been met, no one has been selfish, and they have honored God in their marriage. I should make my spouse's needs my utmost concern all the while eagerly surpassing the interest for my needs. If my spouse does the same, we have covered all the necessities together. Selflessness is better than selfishness in marriage.

Naturally, you shouldn't bend to something unbiblical. You shouldn't disobey your God to please your spouse. We also must beware of unrealistic expectations with which we could burden our marriages. We each have legitimate limitations. In reality, both of those scenarios are the irregular situations. Most of our issues transpire because of unwillingness – not inability. We are merely trying to get our way.

So, if both of you are needy, expectant, and tired, then someone has to reprioritize his or her needs to make the marriage work. In your great neediness, someone has to draw closer. Who will do it? Let it be you! Don't permit the marital drift to widen because of your selfishness.

In those moments when you can muster up enough selfless obedience to serve your spouse, you resemble Jesus who spent his entire life in service to others (Mark 10:45). He emptied himself to become a servant (Phil. 2:7) to people like me who honestly didn't deserve his attention and affection. He gave himself up (Eph. 5:25) for our salvation and as an example of how we should give ourselves up in our marriages (Eph. 5:32). Don't wait until your spouse becomes deserving of your selflessness to give it away. Christ didn't wait for us to become lovely before he chose to love us. Be like Jesus.

What God has joined together, let no selfishness separate.

3 - Let No Selfishness Separate

READ: Philippians 2:3-4

REFLECT: How are you slipping into selfishness within your marriage?

RESPOND: What specific needs does your spouse have that you could prioritize over your own?

4

Let No Conflict Separate

While conflict is unavoidable in a marriage, it doesn't have to be irreconcilable.

The proximity of marriage guarantees conflicts to transpire between spouses. Unmet expectations lead to harsh words and selfish actions. As a result, hurt feelings further validate isolation and retaliation. Every relationship experiences this progression, but it is especially damaging in a marriage.

**The person who knows you the closest
is often able to hurt you the deepest.**

Hurt inflicted by a spouse is uniquely painful. A thousand other people could do things to cause you discomfort, but the same type of attacks from your spouse can cause you uniquely personal devastation. Instead of dealing with the hurt healthily, we often volley further harm back in the direction of our spouse. We justify our actions based on the damage our spouse's actions caused. We vindicate our words as defensive tactics to the rhetorical onslaught from our spouse. Instead of being marked by forgiveness, many marriages thrive on retaliation.

The believer should not respond like the unbeliever. If we have indeed experienced the love and grace of Jesus, then our response mechanisms must surrender to his lordship. Realizing that what feels right may not be right, we have to respond to conflict differently if we desire a different kind of marriage. The forgiveness of Jesus must be the standard by which we mark our marriages. If disputes are guaranteed to happen, then we must learn how to address them biblically. The only way to make your marriage work is if you can forgive your spouse as Jesus has forgiven you. Allow the contagious love of Jesus to run rampant through your home.

> *Let all bitterness and wrath and anger and clamor and slander be put away from you, along with all malice.*
> *Be kind to one another, tenderhearted, forgiving one another, as God in Christ forgave you (Eph. 4:31-32).*

Did you catch that? We are called to forgive one another just as we have been forgiven. Spouses are invited to bear with one another patiently and eagerly forgive one another's mistakes (Col. 3:13).

Conflict will continue to happen in your marriage. So how can we find peace in this life if pain is promised? The only way to find peace in your relationship is to make it. Someone must stop the repercussive pattern of marital payback. You must learn how to get rid of your bitterness and express your forgiveness. In your marriage, you might have so much hurt in the past that you don't know where to start. It is imperative that you deal with yesterday's hurts to avoid tomorrow's conflicts.

Bitterness separates many marriages and will maintain the divide until the couple learns how to employ biblical conflict management. All couples fight, but few couples fight well. Whether you identify your marriage's issues as fights, disagreements, or squabbles, every couple has them. Since we are selfish people, every couple is going to have to work through their issues together. As a couple, you must establish the rules for peacemaking when conflicts do arise. Here are some scriptural ways to handle bitterness and fight through the conflict.

First, never go to bed angry. Scripture teaches that it is acceptable to be angry, but we are not allowed to sin in our anger (Eph. 4:26). Since God's mercies are new every morning (Lam. 3:22-23), we shouldn't ruin tomorrow's potential with today's problems. Deal with today's issues today. There will be plenty to concern yourself with tomorrow (Matt. 6:34).

Second, don't use a "sorry, but." This tactic is subtle but evasive. "I'm sorry I hurt your feelings, but..." These apologies intend to appease your spouse while simultaneously blaming him or her for your actions. When I try to justify my actions, I invalidate my apology. It is more important to be reconciled than it is to be right. Do your part to live at peace (Rom. 12:18) and to pursue it (Heb. 12:14).

Third, don't retract your forgiveness. Since Jesus has forgiven us of so much, we should be eager to forgive one another (Col. 3:13). In that forgiveness, we should forgive like Jesus does (Matt. 6:15-16) removing the trace of sin (Ps. 103:12) and administering the type of love that keeps no record of wrongs (1 Cor. 13:5). Once you forgive your spouse for something, that should be the last time you ever bring it up.

Fourth, no double-teaming. Double-teaming in marriage is when one spouse goes to others for help with marriage issues but never goes to the spouse to work it out. If you have a problem with your spouse, the first person who should know about it should be your spouse. Never involve insignificant others in your relationship with your significant other. Humbly reveal your spouse's faults in private (Matt. 18:15).

Fifth, never play out of bounds. We each have quirks. We each have triggers. We each have areas which we think are out of bounds regarding conflicts. For you, it might be out of bounds for your spouse to walk away during a disagreement or to raise a voice when angered. Some of your words and tactics in communication may not be sinful in of themselves, but due to the wiring of your spouse, they must be off-limits. If your spouse indicates that a word, phrase, expression, action, or mannerism bothers him or her, then take it out of the playbook. Discard it and never use it again. Marriage should teach you to bend to your spouse's desires instead of focusing on your own (Phil. 2:3-4), so find out what frustrates your spouse and stop doing it.

Unfortunately, our spouses often see our worst side. Conflicts in marriage leave battle scars. Knowing that reality, make it a priority to fight against bitterness. Your marriage cannot improve today if you fail to address what happened yesterday. Patiently work through yesterday's conflicts, calmly address today's conflicts, and hopefully, you can avoid some of tomorrow's conflicts.

What God has joined together, let no conflict separate.

4 - Let No Conflict Separate

READ: Ephesians 4:25-32

REFLECT: What are the most common causes of conflict in your marriage?

RESPOND: What fight rules do you need to employ in your marriage to address your conflicts biblically?

5
Let No Miscommunication Separate

Effective communication in marriage is when two people learn to talk with one another rather than just to one another.

While relationships often start with a healthy, rhythmic conversational depth, spouses can reduce communication to pure fact inquiries over time. "How was your day?" "Did you pay the bills?" "Did you remember to help him with his school project?" For a marriage to thrive, you must nurture in-depth dialogue which involves both active listening and authentic speaking.

Intentional communication is vitally important to understand who your spouse is and who your spouse is becoming. If you haven't realized it yet, your spouse is changing. You are changing. And while you may be able to ace the test on the yesteryear version of your spouse, that doesn't guarantee success in understanding the current model. Time and change require a lifelong tutelage on your part.

Communication is the key to an intimate and growing friendship with your spouse.

People cite studies on the communication differences between men and women all the time. Unique differences are noticeable, but stereotypes don't always apply in every situation. Every person communicates differently. One thing is universal – the more that you know your spouse, the better you can love your spouse.

In the Book of Song of Solomon, two lovestruck individuals brag on one another to whoever will listen. The bride makes a brilliant commentary on the relationship regarding what our communication has to do with our intimacy.

> *His mouth is most sweet, and he is altogether desirable. This is my beloved and this is my friend, O daughters of Jerusalem (Song of Solomon 5:16).*

While his mouth might have been full of sweet kisses, I believe she is also relishing in his kind words. She loved what he had to say. His speech made him altogether desirable. The more he spoke, the more she desired him. She highlighted an essential truth that the one she loved was also the one she befriended. She actually brags on her friendship with him to her girlfriends! It is a rare occurrence for a woman to feel the need to express the powerful connection she has with her man due to his strong rhetoric when that type of interaction is usually isolated to girl-talk. Not here. Their sweet communication led them to deeper intimacy.

That type of friendly discussion within marriage doesn't come naturally. Every person has a unique and desired way of connecting with someone else. As different people, sometimes it is hard to get on the same wavelength regarding the conversational habits within the relationship. How do you experience a growing friendship in your marriage cultivated through deep dialogue? You must seek to learn how to connect with your spouse more effectively. To avoid common miscommunication traps, you must realize that in marriage you have different speeds, styles, scenarios, and subjects.

Consider the speed at which you talk with your spouse. Speaking too fast can cause stress and speaking too slow might cause disinterest. Any rate of talking can go too long and encourage a spouse to check out mentally. Talk with your spouse – not to your spouse.

Realize that different styles of communication do exist. Don't force your spouse to become someone he or she isn't. Comparing your spouse to some ideal in your head will prove to be unfruitful. Expecting your spouse to communicate just like you is unfair. Your spouse is meant to compliment you – not clone you. Acknowledge that much of communication is expressed in a nonverbal manner. Sometimes it's not what you say but how you say it.

Study the best scenarios to communicate with your spouse. Sometimes it isn't the content that is the problem but the context. Be realistic that not every situation in life is conducive to effective communication. Seek to connect with your spouse in a scenario that is advantageous to your emotional intimacy. Finding a healthy balance can encourage a healthy marriage. Maybe he needs margin after work. Perhaps she needs some time to process. Possibly a walk around the neighborhood would help both of you. Evaluate the best context for communication and strive for that.

Talk about subjects that engage your spouse. If he or she seems thoroughly checked out, it might be because they have no clue or care about the subject matter you often present. If your communication feels more like a lecture than a discussion, it might be due to a poor selection of topics. If the conversation is always one-sided, your spouse can lose interest in not only the dialogue but also you. One thing I know is that all people love to talk about themselves. Have you asked your spouse a question about him or her while showing genuine interest in an area of his or her passion?

It is entirely acceptable to communicate differently than your spouse as long as you are still talking. Don't be obliviously detached from your spouse's needs or reluctantly dishonest about your wellbeing. Let your spouse off the hook if he or she doesn't communicate like you. You might learn from each other if you would allow it. Amidst the differences, realize that you do have the right to express your need for improvement regarding your conversational patterns. Even in that, be careful how you say what you say.

As you talk about serious issues and silly occurrences, you will learn how to communicate at a more consistent level with your spouse. Your spouse should be both your beloved and friend. If you can't love someone you don't know, then you better get to know your spouse. Since our mouths can do good or evil, work to make your speech a blessing to God and for your spouse (James 3:10).

What God has joined together, let no miscommunication separate.

5 - Let No Miscommunication Separate

READ: James 3:3-12

REFLECT: Would your spouse view your speech as more of a blessing or a curse?

RESPOND: How does your spouse communicate most naturally? How could you selflessly initiate conversation topics that are significant to him or her?

6

Let No Disrespect Separate

Since men need significance in their lives, God calls wives to submit to their husbands.

One of the most-often used and most-often misunderstood passage in Scripture regards Paul's instruction on the need for wives to submit to their husbands and for husbands to love their wives. Our culture disdains such language, but our culture isn't the most exceptional example of successful long-term commitment either, so let's give Scripture a look anyway. The wisdom of the Word is far more steady than the wisdom of this world.

To understand the passages on submission, we need to study them in light of the Bible's entire context. God created Adam from dust and then Eve from Adam. Why was Eve created? God said, "It is not good that the man should be alone; I will make him a helper fit for him" (Gen. 2:18). Process the intentional weight of those words. God made everything with his words until he makes one creation in his own image (Gen. 1:27). He creates these two with his very own hands (Gen. 2:7). If God called all the previous creations "good," then Adam and Eve should be very good. Instead, he looks at Adam before sin ever entered the world and said that he is not good. He is alone. God's response is to create him a helper in Eve.

It's remarkable that being labeled a helper has somehow turned into a derogatory designation. Jesus called the Holy Spirit – the third person of the Trinity – our Helper (John 14:26). If the Holy Spirit of God is labeled as our Helper, how could that ever be a negative moniker? God was completely aware that Adam and Eve both needed help, and he was gracious enough to give them one another.

God created Adam first. The order is not about prominence but position. Adam wasn't more special than Eve. Scripture teaches that while there are differences between male and female, neither one is inherently greater than the other (Gal. 3:28). Adam wasn't better than Eve, but he was before Eve. Somebody had to come first. Since Adam was first, God gave Adam the one commandment before Eve was around. Scripture does not record God giving Eve that instruction. So either he told her that rule behind the scenes or expected Adam to deliver – not command – the expectation to his wife. Adam wasn't commanding his wife; he was sharing God's command with her.

Satan approaches Eve with a temptation to go against that commandment. Throughout the whole conversation, it appears as if Adam is nowhere to be seen, but apparently, Eve either asserts herself, Adam is extremely passive, or both. After their rebellion, God punishes all parties, but Eve's punishment has much to do with the concept of submission.

> *"Your desire shall be contrary to your husband,*
> *but he shall rule over you" (Gen. 3:16).*

It's almost as if in this courtroom sentencing that God is insinuating that Eve had pushed her own agenda. The tension for control was real. While the ideal scenario should be of her husband shepherding her, loving her, and leading her, now he will rule over her. If he struggles to lead due to inadequacy in himself or a sense of inferiority from his wife, he will try to reestablish his presence by the size of his voice, body, or personality. Unfortunately, these early words in Genesis foretell real marital struggles throughout the generations.

As we arrive in the New Testament, the Apostle Paul instructs wives to submit to their husbands. Out of all the commands he could have given, why did he give this one? God knows that disrespect will emasculate a man quicker than anything else in the world. If a woman regularly expresses disrespecting thoughts, attitudes, and words, her husband's demeanor and outlook began to crumble slowly. A disrespectful wife has a unique capability to cripple her husband emotionally.

Acknowledging the fact that men need relational respect, what does Scripture command? Wives, submit to your husbands. Show him respect. Your gentle spirit can change him for the better (1 Pet. 3:4).

Submission has nothing to do with inferiority.
Submission has everything to do with significance.

Ladies, if you haven't noticed, the men in your life have ego problems. They like to be first. They love to be the best at something. Everything in the world is the way it should be when someone recognizes them as the shining pinnacle of manhood.

Much of that can turn unhealthy, but some of that is due to how God made men. God created men to desire significance. Men will go looking for importance in a woman, a job, or a hobby. No matter where they go looking for significance, rest assured, they will find it somewhere. So out of all the places they could go searching for it, is it that bad if they find significance in the marriage relationship? Submission implies showing respect. A submissive wife encourages her husband, loves to listen to her husband, and takes delight in his leadership. What woman wouldn't want to have a man worth following?

If a husband finds significance in his wife,
he doesn't have to look for it anywhere else.

Often, women look at this passage for what it means to them and not what it means to their husbands. That's the danger of any teaching on marriage. We always hope the other person is listening. We justify our actions saying that we would do this if only our spouse would do that. This passage's focus is not to take away anything from women, but it is an invitation for women from God to partner with him to build significance in their husbands.

How could you lovingly submit to your husband? It might be as simple as asking him for his preference on something. You could do it by encouraging him for the things that he does that often go unnoticed. Approach him with a concern and convince him of how much you appreciate his wisdom. Your husband will never become the man you want him to be by telling him all the things he fails to be.

What God has joined together, let no disrespect separate..

6 - Let No Disrespect Separate

READ: 1 Peter 3:1-6

REFLECT: What words and actions show disrespect to your husband?

RESPOND: What are some ways you can show him honor today?

7
Let No Indifference Separate

The level of a man's sacrifice for his wife determines the amount of security she feels in their marriage.

Since Adam's passive refusal to get involved in the Garden's temptation inadvertently led the first home towards sin (Gen. 3:6, 17), men have seemed unfortunately plagued with an inability to provide consistent leadership in marriage and parenting. Instead of being awed by their pioneering initiative, many wives feel disappointed by the lack of drive in their husbands for the things that matter most. Men are known for being driven by pathetic pursuits rather than godly goals. Instead of receiving a committed type of love from their husbands, wives unfortunately receive a passive kind of indifference – a lack of interest, concern, or sympathy for their needs.

> **Many marriages fail simply because husbands do not know how to love their wives.**

Due to our culture's depiction of love, many men feel as if they cannot accomplish what their wives expect of them. An abstract, emotional disposition is hard for a man to provide or even understand. Love stories and love songs claim feelings to be the most accurate thermometer of love. With that explanation, most men feel unable to love a wife because many of them aren't as naturally emotional as their wives. Instead of attempting to connect with their wives on an emotional level, they would much rather do something practical for them. Men are natural fixers but not natural lovers.

Many men fail due to a tragic misunderstanding of what love truly is. Maybe love isn't some fleeting emotion. If God himself is equated with love (1 John 4:8), it cannot be a wishy-washy emotion. It must be something more concrete. Your marriage will drastically change if you grasp the fact that the manliest of men to ever walk this earth was the greatest lover of them all.

> **Husbands, love your wives, as Christ loved the church and gave himself up for her (Eph. 5:25).**

The illustration that God chose to use in his Word to show how husbands should love their wives is how Christ loved the Church. He gave himself up for her. In an attempt to make her holy, he died for her. If you ever wanted to know how to love your wife, look no further than how Jesus showed his love for you.

How did Jesus love you? What did he endure through his crucifixion? Did Jesus deserve that treatment? Embracing the undeserving punishment, he came with joy eagerly looking for that cross (Heb. 12:2). How could anyone intentionally move towards a tortuous execution device? What kind of rationale could he possess to do the unthinkable? He would gladly experience pain so that the one he loved didn't have to endure it. That's how husbands are supposed to love their wives.

> **The level of a man's sacrifice for his wife determines the amount of security she feels in their marriage.**

If you started loving your wife like Christ loved the Church, what would change? You would begin to realize that you are not dying *to* her but *for* her. You sacrifice. You pour yourself out. You love like Jesus – even when she doesn't deserve it.

Many men struggle with loving their wives because of their wives' disrespect. Citing her actions as a justifier, a husband blames her for his inability and unwillingness to love her as is required. Would you like to apply that reasoning to your relationship with God? If Jesus dealt with us the way that many of us deal with our spouses, we would never have received love, forgiveness, or salvation. We would have been eternally condemned in our sins because of our inability to provide any worthiness in ourselves.

Men will fail to love when they surrender to a feminized version of love. There's nothing about a willing sacrifice on a rugged cross that should ever castrate a man. Love doesn't weaken a man; it strengthens him. The greatest of men who ever lived was led like a lamb to the slaughter and did not even open his mouth (Is. 53:7). He endured horrific punishment due to an all-consuming love for his bride. Jesus loved us while we were still unlovely (Rom. 5:8).

While the call for women to submit to their husbands is challenging, the standard for men to love their wives in the same manner that Jesus loved us is breathtakingly overwhelming. In our context, the charge to the women seems shocking. In the original audience, the command to the men was counter-cultural. Men lived in their separate corners of the house and could not be disturbed. They had rights to do with their wives and children whatever they wanted to do. Paul's charge for men to love their wives served as a provocatively shocking statement.

It still is today. If your marriage is to work, men must be like Christ. Men – have your attitudes like Jesus (Phil. 2:5) by putting your wives' needs ahead of your own (Phil. 2:3-4). Don't be harsh with them (Col. 3:19). Live with them in an understanding way or God won't even listen to your prayers (1 Pet. 3:7). Did you catch that? If you don't listen to your wife, God won't listen to you! When our Heavenly Father entrusts his precious princesses into our loving care, he has serious expectations.

If you are still looking for a practical way to fight indifference and truly love your wife, let me give you a clear step – wash your wife in the water of the Word (Eph. 5:26). In Paul's description of sanctification, he instructed husbands to point wives to the Word in the same way Jesus did for the church. That means you should learn the Word in your home so you can lead by the Word in your home. Live only by its principles. To do that, you must prioritize the Bible in your life.

Your wife's submission to you will be simple since you will be submitting to the Word. A wife's submission to a biblical husband is merely a submission to the Bible. Men - you can't lead others in the Word if you don't know the Word. Lead by being led. Love by being loved.

What God has joined together, let no indifference separate.

7 - Let No Indifference Separate

READ: Ephesians 5:25-33

REFLECT: As a man, how are you passive in your home?

RESPOND: What ways could you sacrifice for your wife to provide security for her?

8

Let No Expectation Separate

Unrealistic or unclear expectations in marriage can lead to unforgiving and unwilling spouses.

If you live with someone long enough, he or she will let you down. It's inevitable. As you date someone, you can spot his or her blemishes. Once you marry, your proximity to the flaws exasperates the issues. What used to be annoying becomes irreconcilable. The reason these annoyances are so frustrating is that you had such high expectations for this person. You believed you were getting a spouse who was very close to being put together. In your mind, you should be able to determine the issues within the first few months, buff out those blemishes, and you would be set to go with a new and improved model destined to withstand the test of time. It didn't take you long to realize how complicated that process will prove to be.

Instead of clarifying or simplifying expectations, many people will analyze the meaning of their frustration dangerously. Instead of dealing with the problem, people begin to entertain the possibility that the spouse is the problem. If one feels letdown and depleted, he or she will start to regret the relationship. If the spouse seems unfixable, a potential replacement becomes the subtle or blatant goal.

When your spouse fails to meet your expectations, you begin to question if you married the wrong person. Many people claim that unmet expectations are the problem within their marriage. If they could go back and press rewind, they would have made different decisions and would be in a different place today. Due to rising conflicts in marriages, people think that the problem must be the person. It might not be that you married the wrong person, but that each of you hasn't been made right yet.

Do you believe there is that one particular person for you? Fairy tales taught us that certain princes and princesses are destined to be together. Entertainment taught us that there was that one specific person out there uniquely designed for each of us. The church taught us that God's will was wrapped up in that one person fashioned just for us. So, if all those scenarios are correct, why are so many couples despairingly disappointed in their marriages?

Imagine we simplified the world to an island of 100 people with exactly 50 men and 50 women. The setting is perfect for every person to have a spouse, but we have to make sure that the right person gets the right spouse. Simple enough in theory, but what if one person makes one mistake? What if Man #1 was supposed to marry Woman #51 but instead married Woman #82? Due to this mistake, all other 49 marriages are now potentially doomed to fail! One unfortunate pairing led to the downfall of the entire island.

While that scenario might seem extreme, it is relatively accurate regarding how we process dysfunctional marriages. Expand that island back out to the population of the world right now, and you will see how just one incorrect pairing has now given every other marriage an impossible scenario to succeed. The issue might not be that you married the wrong person but that you haven't dealt with that person in the right way. The health of your marriage can't be dependent upon the correct selection of other unions. Surely we aren't destined to fail. Maybe we have misunderstood the will of God. If you are wondering if you missed the will of God in marrying your spouse, let me clarify your situation.

Once you married your spouse, it became God's will that you remain married to your spouse.

When a man and a woman enter into a marital covenant, that marriage is God's will. He is for that marriage. As believers, we fight against the ignorance of this world by discerning the will of God which are those things that are good and acceptable and perfect (Rom. 12:2). Giving thanks for the spouse you have is God's will for you (1 Thess.

5:18). God's will is for you to grow in Christ and not give into sexual pursuits with someone who is not your spouse (1 Thess. 5:3). God's will is wrapped up in you staying faithful to your spouse and working out the issues present in the marriage. By living obediently to Scripture's expectations, you are fulfilling God's good will which can silence foolish people in their ignorant opposition to the ways of the Lord (1 Pet. 2:15).

Therefore do not be foolish, but understand what the will of the Lord is (Eph. 5:17).

The will of God is for you to stay married. It doesn't mean that it will be easy, but isn't it clarifying to know God is for this union? Since you are intended to stay married, you must start addressing your expectations of one another.

If your expectations are being unmet, you must determine why and adjust your perspective. Most marriages struggle due to unrealistic or unclear expectations. Unrealistic expectations are those demands you make of your spouse of which he or she is incapable of providing. You might be expecting your spouse to give the type of stability and meaning that only God can provide. Putting your husband or wife as an idol is damaging to both of you.

Unclear expectations are those that your spouse could meet if you would merely express them. I have realized that many marital frustrations are merely unspoken requests which could be remedied if someone would just articulate the issue. You didn't marry a mind reader. Don't fault him or her for that. Clarify what you need. Don't punish your spouse as if he or she is unwilling when in reality your spouse merely is unaware.

Whether it is unrealistic or unclear expectations, realize that you are setting your spouse up for failure. He or she can't address what is impossible or vague. Remove the idea that you got the wrong person. Don't lower your standards but simplify and clarify them. In your quest to make your needs known, don't forget about the ones your spouse has present as well. Are you willing to address those needs?

What God has joined together, let no expectation separate.

8 - Let No Expectation Separate

READ: Romans 12:1-2

REFLECT: How do the world's expectations and the Word's expectations of marriage differ? What is God's perfect will for your marriage?

RESPOND: What unrealistic expectation do you need to lower? What unclear expectation do you need to communicate?

9
Let No Past Separate

Couples who cannot reconcile their pasts will never be able to enjoy their future.

When a newlywed couple moves into their first home, it is a time of joyous excitement. Newfound responsibilities are embraced readily due to the joy of being able to welcome them together. They move in all types of furniture, clothes, decorations, and mementos. Among all the items, some have been purchased, and some have been inherited. With every piece, there is a story. One of the most challenging steps is figuring out how to take the husband's stuff and the wife's stuff and somehow miraculously make it into their stuff.

Just like the newness of sharing a home, a married couple attempts to share life together in a brand new way. Each spouse brings plenty of things into the relationship. We all come with baggage – good, bad, or indifferent. The husband and wife both bring a story or a scar from every experience. You are unable to understand new occurrences in your marriage as a couple without interpreting them through old experiences in your past as individuals.

If you mishandle your past, you will misinterpret your present and misdirect your future.

You mishandle your past when you fail to deal with it. Even though it is painful to go back through failures and frustrations, you must address yesterday's hurts if you are to experience tomorrow's joys. If you fail to deal with the past, you will dangerously misinterpret current experiences. You overreact to the situation at hand because of backlogged pain. All of this will lead to a misdirected future because of the frantic pace you swerve through life trying to avoid any remembrance of what made you who you are today. You can't renew your marriage if you don't redeem your past.

The problem with our pasts is that they are broken. For those of us who have experienced relatively easy lives compared to others, we still have moments and experiences that have changed who we are. Hits along the way have knocked us down repeatedly. Sometimes we are jostled by others, and sometimes we stumbled because of our own mistakes. All of those events in the past have altered how we operate today. So if those problems of the past have knocked us down repeatedly, how are supposed to respond?

> *For the righteous falls seven times and rises again,*
> *but the wicked stumble in times of calamity (Prov. 24:16).*

I would assume God's Word would equate someone who falls seven times as unrighteous, but this proverb teaches the complete opposite. God considers this person as righteous due to one simple truth – the resolve to rise after falling. The wicked keep stumbling and can't establish themselves upon their feet. The righteous keep stumbling but continue to rise each time. God is not as concerned with how many times you fall but how many times you get back up.

I realized early in marriage that I never responded to my wife based solely on what she said or did. I noticed that something small could somehow turn big quickly. How could that be? It's because we filter every one of our responses through our past experiences. Previous circumstances layer every situation. I'm not just responding to that situation at that moment, I am responding to everything leading up to that situation at that moment. The particular scenario didn't deserve that layered of a response. Our pasts have a way to amplify our feelings and multiply our comebacks.

Don't make your spouse pay for mistakes he or she didn't commit. Don't make your spouse pay for the mistakes you committed. Don't make your spouse pay for mistakes you have forgiven.

If your spouse didn't commit the hurt, don't make him or her pay for the damage. The past can dominate your marriage by unresolved conflict from other relationships. Whether your family, friends, or former relationships caused the pain, unforgiven offenses will cause unwarranted frustrations. In many cases, the offender isn't still around, but the offended still wants to get back at him or her. It's not fair to make your spouse be the fall guy or gal.

Don't make your spouse pay for your issues either. Stop giving him or her the bill for what you broke. Just because you fell and are embarrassed or devastated by that fact doesn't mean that you need to blame your spouse for your poor decisions. An inability to acknowledge complete forgiveness from God for our sins will cause you to be bitter, cold, and distant. Your spouse needs today's you and not yesterday's you. Deal with your issues in the past and keep them there.

You haven't forgiven your spouse for the past offenses if you continually bring them up. Giving forgiveness lip-service is not helpful to a marriage if you maintain a level of bitterness that you consider to be advantageous to your agenda. Holding a grudge reveals that I believe Jesus' blood is sufficient to forgive my sins against God but not enough to forgive your offenses committed against me. Forgive like Jesus.

If you notice, all three of these scenarios need the same thing – forgiveness. Whether it's offering forgiveness or accepting forgiveness, most situations in our past revolve around our inability to experience it. We are even taught by Jesus to pray that God would "forgive us our debts, as we also have forgiven our debtors" (Matt. 6:12). Do I really want to pray that God would show me the kind of grace that I have shown others?

In Matthew 18:21-35, Jesus taught a parable about forgiveness. A peasant was forgiven a debt that equaled about 200,000 years of salary by his master and yet unwilling to forgive a fellow peasant about one-third of a year's salary. Seems shocking? It is! And we do it every time we refuse to forgive someone and move past our past. You have been forgiven a massive debt incurred by your sin, why not take some of that grace and share it with your spouse?

What God has joined together, let no past separate.

9 - Let No Past Separate

READ: Matthew 18:21-35

REFLECT: What issues from the past are still affecting you presently?

RESPOND: Where do you need to offer forgiveness or request forgiveness?

10

Let No Parent Separate

If you are not careful, your relationship with your parents can threaten your relationship with your spouse.

While marriage opens a new and glorious chapter in one's life, it also closes a significant preceding chapter. When we were married, the excitement as we departed for our honeymoon was unrivaled. But somewhere among the bubbles being blown on us as we rushed to our getaway vehicle, my bride caught her mother's eyes and realized a simple yet life-changing truth: she wasn't returning home when we got back.

The location of the home had just changed. All the years of depending upon her parents' strength and provision were replaced with a simple, "I do." Her address had changed. She had a new last name. Her immediate family changed at the very moment when I kissed the bride.

Depending upon life circumstances at the time of marriage, some people's departure from the nest can be sudden, and others can be subtle. Like an athlete who was drafted by one team and traded to another, it is hard to get used to another jersey and a different brand. Such a change is all-encompassing. Whether it happens over time or in the blink of an eye, it's a significant adjustment.

Regarding your parents, there are two equal marital dangers: dishonoring abandonment or reluctant detachment.

Dishonoring abandonment is when a couple gets married and blatantly ignores their parents. Through what they say and how they say it, the newlyweds seem ungrateful for what their parents have done and unconcerned about how their parents are doing. While the marriage relationship must change the relationship with both sets of parents, it doesn't mean those relationships should be abandoned casually or callously.

Reluctant detachment is equally as dangerous. If one or both spouses are unwilling to alter their relationship priorities, the marriage cannot be healthy. If one's parents are more valued than one's spouse, relational intimacy is impossible to obtain. An unwillingness to have a normal priority of one's spouse will create jealousy, bitterness, and resentment. Not only will the disregarded spouse feel jaded in the marriage, but the relationship with the spouse's family can slowly turn toxic.

Even while it seems difficult to obtain, there is a healthy balance. When you start your family with your spouse, it doesn't mean that you have to end your family with your parents. It will be different though. It has to be different, or your marriage cannot thrive. In the early pages of Scripture, God provides explicit commands to adult children regarding how to obtain this balance regarding their relationship with their parents. Scripture commands adult children to leave and yet to honor their parents.

> *Therefore a man shall leave his father and mother and hold fast to his wife, and the two shall become one flesh (Eph. 5:31).*

In leaving your parents, you are committing to a level of exclusive oneness with your spouse that should not be rivaled by any other earthly relationship. In describing the first husband and wife, Scripture teaches that a man should leave parents and cleave to spouse (Gen. 2:24). Adam and Eve didn't even have earthly parents, so why was this statement written? It was written for every couple after them including us. The marital union must be fundamentally distinct from every other relationship in every possible way.

Too many marriages never experience oneness because they still depend upon the emotional, financial, and relational support from at least one set of parents. Good intentions can lead to wrong expressions. Prolonging your marriage's detachment from your parent's help fails to provide you with a sense of oneness in your marriage and offers an opportunity for your parents to treat you as immature children who still need them. You can never fully stand on each other when you are being propped up by your parents. At some point, you must learn to rely on one another for every critical area of life.

In honoring your parents, you are committing to an intentional level of respect that values your parents' God-given roles throughout every stage of your life. The Ten Commandments contain four vertical commandments (how I relate to God) and six horizontal commandments (how I relate to others). Out of all the critical commandments, the first horizontal command is to "honor your father and mother, that your days may be long" (Ex. 20:12). The command to honor one's parents preceded the command not to murder. When we honor our parents, we honor God. God didn't give this command only to the preschoolers assembled at Mt. Sinai. An 80-year-old Moses first heard this command, and he was expected to obey it.

Even when it is difficult to honor the person of your parent, always honor the position of your parent. Show honor even when they disappoint you. As married adults, you are not called to obey your parents, but that doesn't mean you need to disrespect them if they still try to coddle you or command you. As far as it depends on you, live at peace with them (Rom. 12:18).

Is it possible to leave and yet honor? Without a doubt! God wouldn't give us both commands as if one canceled the other one out. You can and should do both.

Learn to respect your parents without relying on your parents.

Look to your parents for insight but don't depend upon them for instruction. You can administer deep hurts when you choose your parents' opinions over your spouse's. If you have a parent that is trying to get too involved in your family's affairs, put an end to it for the sake of your marriage but do it in a way that honors your parent and glorifies the Lord.

What God has joined together, let no parent separate.

10 - Let No Parent Separate

READ: Read Genesis 2:18-25

REFLECT: Do you feel like your relationship with your parents is in a safe position as it relates to your relationship with your spouse?

RESPOND: How can you ensure your spouse regarding his or her priority over every other one of your relationships?

II

Let No In-Laws Separate

When you marry a person, you inherit a family.

Whether or not you realized it, your marriage came as a packaged deal. Without warning, you just added a slew of people that you now consider family. Each side probably has both functional and dysfunctional family members, and now you have united them all together for a lifetime. Your spouse's family becomes your own. Your own family becomes your spouse's. Regardless of how great they may be, more people creates more problems. If you're not careful, it doesn't take long before your in-laws can feel like outlaws.

The marriage union is distinct from any other relationship. Once you share vows, your previous immediate family changes in an instant, but they do not just go away. Not only do you continue connections with them, but you just inherited an entirely separate group of people as a family who probably does things opposite of how your childhood family does things. It is obvious why frustration with in-laws can increase very quickly.

> **When you marry someone, you inherit**
> **all the good and bad of that person's family.**

The only couple in the history of Mankind who didn't have to worry about bringing baggage into the marriage was Adam and Eve. With no parents preceding them, their marriage union should have been simple. Have you ever found it interesting that the description of their union includes this statement:

"This is why a man leaves his father and mother
and bonds with his wife, and they become one" (Gen. 2:24).

The first marriage didn't need that piece of advice, so why was it included? Every marriage after that would rise and fall depending upon how well they could apply that truth. God knew the danger associated when someone takes priority over a spouse. People can become resentful towards their in-laws when a spouse essentially chooses familial closeness over spousal oneness.

A wife feels threatened when her husband listens to his mother more than he does to her. A husband feels betrayed when his wife tells his wrongdoings to her family. Conflict arises when family traditions and holiday plans take precedence over marital consideration. Petty annoyance with one's in-laws can turn into full-blown marital strife if not dealt with healthily.

You must learn to prioritize your marriage without
idolizing your side of the family or demonizing
your spouse's side of the family.

Idolizing your side of the family is when you put your family's traditions on a pedestal under which all practices of other families are deemed as inferior. Hopefully, you view your memories with your family as something worth noting and repeating, but if you are not careful, you can cause a non-essential issue to carry an essential weight. Your family is great, but it doesn't mean that they are perfect.

Demonizing your spouse's side of the family is when you show disgust of how they do what they do. Instead of treating the family as merely different than yours, you reveal an aghast demeanor to how they operate. Whether words, looks, or actions show it to the family or it is shared privately with your spouse, it seeks to communicate your disapproval. Even if it seems as simple observations that you share, inherently, you are demeaning some of the most important people in your spouse's life.

Problems can originate from your side of the family or your spouse's side of the family, but you need to resolve that they won't interfere with your marriage. The health of your marriage can often be gauged by the way you speak of "your" family. If "my" family wants to do this, but "your" family wants to do that, it appears that drama is inevitable because you honestly don't know who your family is right now.

If you don't live as though your spouse is your closest family member, your marriage cannot thrive. If you don't see your spouse as "your" family, then is it unsurprising you are experiencing such turmoil within your own home? You have an us vs. them mentality, and somehow you have placed your spouse on the opposing team. Once married, you must embrace the reality that your spouse's people are now your people (Ruth 1:16).

While oneness in marriage is an undeniable theological concept and reality, the practical side of dealing with in-laws can be challenging. How should this truth flesh out in your family? You must seek to have the healthiest relationship possible with your in-laws while acknowledging the unique relationship that your spouse still has with them. There is just more history there, and failure to recognize that will lead to continual frustration.

Most people have realized that you can say something about your side of the family, but if your spouse said the same thing about them, you could quickly become offended. You can say less about your spouse's family than he or she does and it carries a more severe consequence. For whatever reason, it's acceptable to talk about your mother but unacceptable for someone else to do it. While you continue to nurture your marital oneness, you must learn how to embrace these other family members and not anger your spouse in the process.

The simplest way to do this is to apply Scripture to how you speak about your in-laws with your spouse. "Know this, my beloved brothers: let every person be quick to hear, slow to speak, slow to anger" (James 1:19). When it comes to your in-laws, 1) be quick to hear from your spouse about his or her feelings, 2) be slow to speak your first feelings regarding the situation, and 3) be slow to anger as you work through the issue.

What God has joined together, let no in-laws separate.

11 - Let No In-Laws Separate

READ: James 1:19-21

REFLECT: Who on your side of the family causes the most stress to your spouse? Who on your spouse's side of the family creates you the most tension?

RESPOND: How can you prioritize your spouse over your side of the family? How can you honor your spouse's side of the family? What do you appreciate about your in-laws? How can you express that to your spouse?

12

Let No Child Separate

Prioritizing your children can lead to neglecting your spouse.

We must keep children in their proper place. There are dangers on every side. Some people put so much stock into their parenting that the success of the children become the standard of the parent's worth. Unhealthy attachment can cause parents to attempt to live vicariously through their children. To the other extreme, some adults ignore and disregard their children as nuisances to be avoided. If the verbalized anticipation of parenting is to get the kids out of the house, children begin to question their value in the eyes of their parents.

I can remember the unbridled joy when I became a father. As our tribe continued to increase through the years, I felt like the most blessed man in the world. I quickly realized that close relationships and random strangers both love to give you their thoughts regarding children. Somewhere along the way, I almost felt that to have a conversation about parenting required an exhausted admission that I "sure do have my hands full." In reality, I do have my hands full – full of blessings. Regardless of what current culture and other people depicts, children are a blessing and not a burden.

> *Behold, children are a heritage from the LORD,*
> *the fruit of the womb a reward (Ps. 127:3).*

Children are priceless gifts from the LORD (Ps. 127:3) and should be treated as such. Scripture teaches that the more children one has, the more blessings one has (Ps. 127:5). Don't listen to the cultural naysayers who are critical of God's gifts.

Many couples desire children but struggle with why they can't become pregnant. While many couples struggle with infertility or suffer from the pain of miscarriage, those hardships cannot stop you from becoming parents. Through the beautiful process of adoption, God can make any couple experience the joy of parenthood. The concept of parenting is so glorious that only God should get the credit for however a child comes into the loving care of a home. Whether the child comes into the family through birth or adoption, only God can give such a gift as a child and only does he have the unique ability to create a family!

While children are one of God's greatest gifts, a subtle yet dangerous trap is for parental demands to hinder marital unity. In every stage of parenting, the requirements are significant. The amount of care, attention, affection, time, and resources that the tiniest members of your family require can be stifling. If not careful, a blessing from the marriage will take priority over the marriage.

After you have experienced the first sleepless night of parenting, your entire world forever changes. To be an intentional parent will cause you to invest a significant amount of physical and emotional reserves in your children. Through all stages of parenting, you can feel as if you are a maid, policeman, chauffeur, counselor, tutor, short-order chef, mentor, and so much more.

Unfortunately, many marriages end in divorce once the nest is emptied of children. So many people anticipate this time as an opportunity to rekindle and reconnect, and yet frequently, there is nothing left of the marriage to show. After the last child departs home and begins the journey to independence, many couples who appeared to have it altogether call it quits all of a sudden. In reality, these marriages have been on a steady drift for at least eighteen years.

If the child becomes the sole shared experience within a marriage, the marriage will be over as soon as that child leaves home.

When raising children becomes the sole focus of the home, the marriage will suffer. When spouses become nothing more than business partners dedicated to the job of maturing children, the relationship is in trouble. Raising children requires an enormous amount of work, but it can't be the only shared work in the home. Couples experience this drift all the time. The dad gives any remaining time after work to the children. The mom pours all she has into covering the needs and the wants of the children's lives. Along the way, they lose sight of one another. These two parents circle each other as co-workers who don't know how to exist once the "clients" are gone.

You must find a balance. You must find room to nurture your children after you have cherished your spouse. While the parent/child relationship is unparalleled in uniqueness, there is only one person you are called to be one with – your spouse.

I remind my children often, "We were together before you got here, and we are still going to be together once you are gone." While your relationship as a parent never changes, your role will change. Contrastingly, your marriage should never have a graduation period. Your relationship with your child should decrease in dependence while your relationship with your spouse should increase in dedication.

One litmus test to reveal the danger in your home is to ask the question: Did I feel more like a spouse or a parent today? If you feel like the role of parent dwarfed the role of spouse, you need to make some changes quickly. I know your children have needs and you want to show them your love, but don't neglect one of the most critical things you can do for your children.

One of the most significant ways you can love your child is by prioritizing your spouse.

As you lovingly teach your children that your spouse comes first, you are modeling a healthy marriage for them, maintaining emotional security for them, and maturing your marriage right before them. Never neglect the task of shepherding your children in the ways of the Lord (Prov. 22:6; Eph. 6:4), but never forget that one of the primary ways you can fulfill that is by loving their other parent.

What God has joined together, let no child separate.

12 - Let No Child Separate

READ: Psalm 127:1-5

REFLECT: Based on your thoughts and actions, have you embraced the role of spouse or parent more recently?

RESPOND: What can you do today to prioritize your marriage over your parenting?

13
Let No Friendship Separate

Any friendship that detracts from your marriage is an unhealthy one.

It has become expected to say that your spouse also serves the role of your best friend. While some people legitimately mean that, others use the trite phrase in an attempt to manufacture relational weight. You don't have to verbalize who your best friend is – you show it every day by the direction of who you communicate with, the depth of what you communicate about, and the duration of how long you communicate.

When something exciting or tragic happens, who do you contact first? You reveal your natural direction at that moment. Do you want to share it with your spouse or is there someone else closer with whom you need to share it?

What relationship has the most significant emotional and conversational depth? In many marriages, basic facts are shared, but honest dialogue can be lacking. Many people have someone else that knows the person better than the spouse. More intimate details, thoughts, and feelings can be expressed with a friend rather than a spouse.

The duration of communication shares much about a friendship as well. When someone has that friend with whom he or she can talk with for hours yet struggles to find conversational content with one's spouse, that admission might reveal a deeper emotional connection exists with someone other than the spouse. Can you communicate easily?

Friendships are important. Yes, men will sometimes open up to other men, and women can often talk with other women for longer. None of those things are wrong, but you must be careful.

You and your spouse need healthy and balanced friendships with other people to have a healthy relationship with one another.

An extreme position in either direction is dangerous. A controlling personality unwilling to allow a spouse to enjoy other friendships will significantly frustrate his or her companion. A socialite who is too busy and too popular to connect with his or her spouse will push the marriage to the side.

Too many strive to find a balance between connecting with healthy friendships while maintaining an exclusive intimacy and bond with your spouse. The Book of Song of Solomon strikes the right chord. At different times, the groom, the bride, and the bridesmaids all have their opportunity to contribute to the conversation. At one place, the bride tells her close friends about the relationship with her man as describing him as one possessing a sweet mouth and making him all the more desirable (SS 5:16).

The bride's best friend has a sweet mouth and a desirable presence. Not only does she consider him her beloved but also her friend. What a powerful combination! Notice that she informs her closest friends who are in the wedding party. She is unashamed to tell the closest companions that a girl can have at the most special moment in her life that there is no friendship like the one she has with her husband. That type of relational intimacy should be the goal of any marriage. You can have both close friends and a more intimate friendship with your spouse. Your spouse should have a love that comes from your very soul – a unique love to any other relationship.

> *Scarcely had I passed them when I found him whom*
> *my soul loves. I held him, and would not let him go*
> *(Song of Solomon 3:4).*

If you aren't careful though, your friendship can eclipse your marriage. How do you know if you are in danger? You are in trouble if you share greater amounts of time, conversations, and experiences with your friend than you do your spouse.

First, watch how you spend your time. Time is like money. If you spend it in on one thing, you can't invest it into another. Scripture teaches that the days are evil and so we must be cautious about how we spend our moments (Eph. 5:15-17). Relational intimacy takes time, and it cannot happen with your spouse if you invest an unhealthy amount of time with your friends. If all of your free time is spent fostering other relationships, your marital intimacy will wane, and your spouse will grow frustrated and discontent.

Second, guard your conversations. You also must be careful how you prioritize your discussions with your friends versus your spouse. In a day, you experience all types of highs and lows. Regardless of how you are wired, some form of verbal communication is needed to process through particular circumstances. Even if the conversation is more natural with a friend than your spouse, you run the risk of emotional separation if you talk about the essential things in your life with people who should come in second place. The subtle danger is that you can confide in a best friend and feel better about the situation and yet you have unknowingly distanced yourself from your spouse. It is beneficial to have friends with whom you can confide but make sure they don't become an unhealthy substitute for your spouse. Don't let anyone take the place of your husband or wife.

Finally, be careful that you share positive experiences with your spouse and not merely your friends. Often, spouses have to walk through challenging circumstances, weighty decisions, and tiring commitments. If you only share the tasks of life together but not the joys of life, you are setting yourself up for a disenfranchised marriage. A friend enjoys you at your happiest moments while sharing some of the greatest laughs, memories, and experiences.

Don't save the happy moments for a friend and the tense moments for a spouse. Ensure that some of those special moments are reserved for your spouse. All healthy friendships will be with those who support your marriage and never threaten your marriage.

What God has joined together, let no friendship separate.

13 - Let No Friendship Separate

READ: Song of Solomon 3:1-5

REFLECT: Is there a friendship that might threaten your spouse?

RESPOND: How can you ensure you spend quality time together with your spouse?

14

Let No Sexual Struggle Separate

Sex is the most unique activity within marriage.

You will talk, share, and enjoy life with many people. You should only have sex with one person. The act of physical union between a husband and a wife is one of the most essential facets of marital oneness. It is not the most critical aspect, but it should not be reduced to a mere physical act that denies its importance to the overall health of the marriage relationship.

As life gets more hectic, it is easy to neglect this component of your marriage. Maintaining physical intimacy is so vitally important because you must ensure that the sexual element of your relationship is prioritized. As a marriage progresses through the years, the unique gift of sex can be underrated. Many marriages disconnect over an increasing lack of intimacy.

> **The lack of prioritized passion in a marriage
> leads to a dangerous disconnect between spouses.**

Did you know that Scripture urges marriages to maintain their sexual relationship? For those who have struggled with reading the Bible, I may have just created a studious student of Scripture out of you. While that may seem shocking, it makes sense if you think about it. Who created sex? God did. If he created sex, don't you think it is wise to approach the owner's manual on how to operate this gift in the best way possible?

Many people imagine God as a cosmic killjoy who doesn't want his children to have any fun or enjoy anything in this life. People have a concept of God that says if something is enjoyable, he probably wouldn't want us to partake in it. That couldn't be further from the truth. Sex is a wonderfully brilliant gift from God.

Sex in marriage can bring about praise (thanking him for such a great gift - James 1:17), procreation (ushering in the wonder of a child's life - Ps. 127:3), pleasure (enjoying the delight of your spouse - Prov. 5:19), and protection (meeting an essential need in your spouse so as to help ensure he or she doesn't go looking to experience it somewhere else - 1 Cor. 7:5).

Let your fountain be blessed, and rejoice in the wife of your youth, a lovely deer, a graceful doe. Let her breasts fill you at all times with delight; be intoxicated always in her love (Prov. 5:18-19).

Scripture unashamedly celebrates the sexual union in marriage. I realize that passages regarding physical and sexual delight found in Proverbs and the Song of Solomon aren't the most quoted portions of Scripture, but we shouldn't neglect them. The Bible isn't timid on the topic of sex. Specifically, the risqué nature of the Song of Solomon caused many Bible interpreters to present another meaning than what seemed to be clear and evident. Instead of approaching the book as a celebration of the unique emotional, spiritual, and sexual union between a husband and wife, people began to think of the message as highlighting Christ's love for his people. If receiving the sensual message of the book and applying it to marriage seemed awkward, I don't know how it makes it any better to think about it as describing Christ's love for us. Maybe marriage is so important that it's reasonable that one book of the Bible out of the sixty-six contained within the canon is dedicated to nurturing the gift of sex within the confines of marriage.

The Bible is full of reminders about the delight to be found in sexual intimacy. Scripture commands spouses not to deprive one another of sex (1 Cor. 7:5). You are intended to view your spouse as beautiful and pleasant, full of all types of delights (SS 7:6). We are called to enjoy life with the one we love (Ecc. 9:9). So, if sex is so important and should be so enjoyable, what is the problem?

Most couples are dangerously disconnected in sexual intimacy due to a lack of priority, a lack of interest, or a lack of concern. If your sex life has a lack of priority, it is probably due to increasing demands in your life. As a family grows, the years seem short but the days seem long. When you finally settle your kids down for bed, and your unfinished tasks are rescheduled or procrastinated until tomorrow, sometimes you don't have an ounce of energy left to give to your spouse. Let me make this simple: You are going to have to find it. If prioritizing passion in your marriage is lacking, I will say something that sounds decidedly unromantic but could prove to be crucial for you: put sex on your calendar. Everything else in your life happens because you plan for it, so decide which days of the week you will prioritize intimacy with your spouse and get back to this significant item of business.

Some couples struggle with intimacy due to a lack of interest. If you are attempting to meet your sexual needs in any other way besides the romantic connection within your marriage, you will not pursue your spouse as intently and as regularly as you should. Don't cheapen God's gift of sex by finding a quick fix in a lustful thought, pornographic image, or flirtatious interactions with another person. Don't let unfair comparison of photoshopped images and sensualized celebrities rob you of the gift of your spouse. Cherish your spouse sexually.

If you struggle with intimacy due to a lack of concern, it is because you might be operating out of a selfish, inconsiderate mindset regarding your spouse's needs. No person has a right to step outside the bounds of marriage to have a sexual need met, but you can significantly help your spouse fight against temptation by eagerly and persistently nurturing this area in your relationship. Every aspect of marriage is about meeting another's needs. Don't make sex all about you, but let care and concern drive your desire to love your spouse in this critical area.

Don't view sex as an isolated physical activity of your marriage but as a central component of your overall intimacy.

What God has joined together, let no sexual struggle separate.

14 - Let No Sexual Struggle Separate

READ: Proverbs 5:15-23

REFLECT: What is hindering your sex life in your marriage?

RESPOND: What can you change to prioritize the sexual fulfillment of your spouse?

15

Let No Secrets Separate

Keeping secrets from your spouse threatens the oneness that marriage was uniquely intended to provide.

Marriage was intended to create a particular type of unity that no other human relationship should ever rival. As God brought Adam and Eve together, they were exposed in every possible way and were utterly peaceful about it. "And the man and his wife were both naked and not ashamed" (Gen. 2:25). This verse naturally reveals the secure nature of their physical relationship with one another, but at an even deeper level, God was showing us that there should be absolutely nothing hidden from our spouses. In our marriages, we should have nothing to cover up and nothing of which to be bashful.

Unfortunately, we bring sin into our marriage like they brought sin into the Garden. What was the direct response to their transgression? They hid from each other (Gen. 3:7) and God (Gen. 3:8) – they did the best they could to cover up. Our situation is no different. Our sins cause us to cover up. Since we have sinned and been sinned against, our trust level is minimal, and we drift towards secrecy rather than honesty. Regardless of how hard we try to keep secrets from others, every secret has a limited shelf life and will eventually be exposed.

> *For God will bring every deed into judgment,*
> *with every secret thing, whether good or evil*
> *(Ecc. 12:14).*

If God knows about our secrets, and every secret will eventually be revealed, wouldn't you rather be the one controlling the information? Wouldn't you prefer to confess than to be caught? Even though a confessional process can be painful, your marriage requires honesty and transparency.

If the content of our secrets are as harmless as we believe, then why are we so fearful of sharing them? You don't have to make it a big deal if you don't think it is a big deal. Any suggestion that the secrets aren't significant reveals the present danger in our hearts of being exposed. If your marriage isn't a safe place to be open, you have already closed your relational intimacy. The very fact that you consider hiding something from your spouse is either because something is unholy or someone is untrustworthy.

If your secret is unholy, that's a red flag that your sin needs to be addressed. There's nothing in secret that God will not bring to light (Luke 8:17). Whatever a man sows, that is precisely what he will reap (Gal. 6:7). You are lying to yourself if you think can handle your sin on your own. You need help, and you won't receive it in secretive isolation.

If you or your spouse is untrustworthy, that is also a serious red flag that needs to be addressed within your marriage. Due to our pasts, we bring significant trust issues into our marriage relationships. You might be married to someone that you are afraid of being honest due to how he or she might handle the truth. If you are concerned that your spouse will treat your honesty with anger, depression, resentment, or estrangement, it can cause you to try to maintain your cover.

In many cases, if you believe your spouse to be an unsafe place to be honest and transparent, you might find yourself opening yourself up to someone else. While a friend can be a healthy option for emotional encouragement, it reveals the state of your marriage if you are more relationally open to a friend than a spouse. It is rarely appropriate to share with someone something you feel that you cannot share with your spouse. It is never appropriate to share with someone of the opposite sex something you aren't sharing with your spouse. The emotional intimacy will be the door through which every other type of intimacy will follow.

A marriage is in trouble when someone knows something significant about you that your spouse doesn't know.

If you keep secrets from your spouse, you will experience devastating consequences. Any part of your life that is unknown causes distrust and disconnection between the two of you. Not only are you growing distant from one another, but the very nature of a secret implies that you are drawing closer to something or someone in the process. Both actions are a simultaneously straightforward movement. Eventually, you have disconnected your spouse from this precious, protected part of your life. If this central area of your life is worth protecting from your spouse, it will eventually be worth to choose the object of the secret over the person of your spouse.

While no one wants personal weaknesses to be exposed, it is better to acknowledge them earlier rather than later. A tiny spark is much more manageable than a raging fire. If someone tries to cover up a secret, it can only lead to more hiding. Lying opens the door for more lying.

When I was once counseling a couple on the brink of divorce, the man who had just had a secret exposed involuntarily wanted his wife to move past the consequences. He claimed that she should be able to forgive and forget, but I informed him that the process would take time. She could have trusted his desire for reconciliation better if he had admitted the sin before being caught in the sin. His secrets caused her continual suspicion.

The easiest way to avoid keeping secrets from your spouse is to avoid doing anything that you need to hide from him or her in the first place. Resolve to be holy because your God is holy (1 Pet. 1:15-16). Put the deeds of the flesh to death (Rom. 8:13), and you will rid yourself of any damaging secrets.

Realizing that we all will make mistakes, don't add another error on top of that one by refusing to be honest. Develop and maintain trust in your marriage relationship at all costs. If you have broken the trust, it will take time to reestablish it. Be patiently willing to do the hard work of reconciliation.

What God has joined together, let no secrets separate.

15 - Let No Secrets Separate

READ: Ecclesiastes 12:13-14

REFLECT: Do you have any secrets that you are keeping from your spouse?

RESPOND: To promote trust, what do you need to confess or address with your spouse?

16

Let No Career Separate

Some couples get married to their work and merely work on their marriage.

Marriage requires time, skill, and commitment. Unfortunately, many relationships don't utilize those elements because they spend them entirely upon their careers. Well-intended spouses can still fail at nurturing marital unity because they have nothing left to give at the end of a tiring workday. Instead of benefiting from your first offerings, he or she may, unfortunately, receive your leftovers. With that priority structure in place, your career may thrive, but your marriage will dissolve.

Don't fool yourself by saying that your provision negates the importance of your presence.

You have a biblical expectation that you will give your family what they need (1 Tim. 5:8). Provision is essential and even God-honoring, but too many people excuse emotional laziness and mental detachment on the fact that their job requires so much of them. While your family undoubtedly benefits from the provision that you acquire through a career, they need your engaged presence even more. They want you more than they want the stuff your job can provide. Your family would rather live with you than live in a bigger house without you.

Since all of us gravitate towards spending additional time on whatever has the highest potential of accomplishment, sometimes marriages struggle because it is easier to be successful at work than it is to be at home. The workplace often provides more concrete benchmarks of success than the homestead can. While many people have tedious tasks at work, family life is an ongoing pursuit with targets that appear to be on the move. If people feel that they are more successful at work, they do not hesitate to bury themselves in those tasks because at least they can daily gauge the measure of their accomplishments.

As our family grew and each member's needs increased at home, my pastoral responsibilities seemed to expand at the same time. Admittedly a driven person in most areas, I assumed I deserved a husband-of-the-year award due to my willingness to help out with anything my wife needed in the evenings and weekends when I was home. During one conversation, my wife ever so gently revealed something to me regarding my commitment to work and family.

While she said it kindly, I will provide you with my summarized synopsis: she would have loved if I displayed the same drive at home that I did at work. Given the demands of our family, she desired to see in our home the same hardworking capability, problem-solving mentality, and the over-and-beyond vitality she saw me commit to my work. I was going all-out for my job and just-enough for my family.

What could tempt a man or a woman to forsake a marriage to prioritize a career? The common temptations are pay, promotion, progress, or praise. The possibility of an increased paycheck has sent many people to justify their lack of time to work on their marriage. The lure of a promotion is a tangible status symbol that can empower a needy individual. Since relationships are hard work and can only see small improvements day to day, the accessible progress available with a job well done can be addictive. Especially if a marriage relationship is weak in the affirmation department, praise received from employers or coworkers can unhealthily fill a gap in a demoralized individual. These temptations can lead a person to prioritize a career over a spouse because the rewards can sometimes come easier.

> *All the toil of man is for his mouth,*
> *yet his appetite is not satisfied (Ecc. 6:7).*

Can you work incessantly and still be unsatisfied? When King Solomon wrote those words, no one could have rivaled his career success. Even among his incredible résumé, he knew that for all the benefits that a job can provide, our core appetites would remain unsatisfied. We need more than what a position can provide. Our eternal souls crave for something far more significant than temporal fruits of our labor. At the end of our lives, we will seek out our relationships and forget about our accomplishments. If you live solely for the commendation that your job can provide, you might miss out on the blessings given from your family (Prov. 23:22; 31:28) and the "well done" supplied by your God (Matt. 25:21).

Killing yourself at your job for the sake of providing for your family makes no logical sense if you lose your family in the process. With the continual advance of technology, our jobs were supposed to become more relaxed and our work hours were supposed to decrease by now, but quite the opposite has happened. It almost seems as if there are forces that are trying to separate the family unit from one another through our jobs. To keep your marriage intact, you must fight against the trend.

Learn how to prioritize your marriage over your career. You must discover how to live in such a way that makes that a reality and convinces your spouse that you mean it. Evaluate how you ascribe value to your marriage while at work and while at home.

You can prioritize your marriage even while you are on the clock. The reality that many of us spend more waking hours around our co-workers than we do our family has caused the rise of the term, "work family." Regardless of how many hours you spend at your job site, you can show your spouse your commitment by working hard during work hours to get off on time, sending messages during the day to affirm your love for your spouse, and leaving notes in his or her path during the day show affirmation.

You can prioritize your marriage while you are off the clock by genuinely being off the clock. Learn how to unplug from work so you can connect with your spouse. Talk about work together but don't stay there. Resist the urge to engage with work demands while at home. The goal is to have a marriage intact when your career is over. That effort must start now.

What God has joined together, let no career separate.

16 - Let No Career Separate

READ: Ecclesiastes 4:4-16

REFLECT: How do you think that your job is affecting your marriage?

RESPOND: What can you adjust in order to be more present with your family when you are absent from work?

17
Let No Busyness Separate

Romance, nurture, and communication takes time.

Unfortunately, time is one of those things that we feel as if we don't have anymore. Our society is obsessed with obtaining immediate results without long-term investments. We want the best things in life to come quick and easy, and yet it rarely happens that way.

With increased advancements, society posited years ago that we would have more free time currently than at any other time in history. Due to such rapid progress, most of us wouldn't have to work as hard or as long, and we would have more opportunities for leisure than we could imagine. The technological revolution continues to increase, and yet it seems as if the opposite is happening. Instead of more time available, we feel as if there is less time to do the things we want or need to do.

Busyness can cause us to idolize our productivity and tempt us to live a lifestyle that seeks independence from God. Many people wear busyness as a badge of honor, and yet it costs us more than we realize. As we give our minutes, hours, days, months, years, and lives away to different pursuits, we can never take back the time invested. The tragedy of how we spend our time is that it is often our marriages that suffer the most.

The one who deserves your best often gets your worst.

How do you know if busyness is affecting your marriage? If you interact with one another more as business partners managing financial responsibilities, household duties, and children's schedules, you might be in danger. If you justify why you can't spend so much time with your spouse due to other relational expectations, your priorities are out of order. If it is a rare occasion for the two of you to carve out time for a simple date, you need to make some changes. If you seem to get agitated with one another easily due to stress, you need to evaluate your existing responsibilities. If you realize that when you actually do find time to spend together, you each live in your own world mentally, emotionally, or technologically, you should be on high alert. Busyness may be robbing your marriage.

> **Look carefully then how you walk, not as unwise but as wise, making the best use of the time, because the days are evil (Eph. 5:15-16).**

If the days are evil, that means that we must be on guard against distractions and pursuits that could rob us of time. To be wise, we must do regular, thorough investigation into how we spend our time. If you have ever sought for the will of God, look no further – it is found in investing your time wisely (Eph. 5:17).

If you allot your time wisely, you will make time for your marriage. We make time for what we love. Ignore the lie that once you get through a particular season of life, you will have time to spend together. Something will always fill your calendar if you let it. If you don't take time to nurture your relationship now, you won't have the relationship to nurture later. Don't allow the most crucial person in your life to receive the leftovers.

For the sake of your marriage, you must reign in your schedule. Having a controlled calendar might mean lesser hours spent on a hobby, fewer activities for your children, or having to say "no" to good things for the sake of your marriage. Just think about how healthy your marriage could be if you invested more quality time into it.

Don't prioritize your schedule, schedule your priorities. If you don't schedule your priorities, someone or something will schedule them for you. When that happens, you spouse invariably will receive the pitiful and insufficient remainder.

If you discover that busyness is endangering your marriage, what should you do? Schedule a daily connection, a weekly date, and a yearly getaway as recurring calendar commitments. Anticipate, plan, budget, prepare, and enjoy these three events for the sake of your marriage.

A daily connection provides you with a short yet regularly intentional time to foster togetherness. This time reserves the right to ban technology, exclude children, exhibit eye-contact, promote touch, and experience reconnection. Find a time during the day to have undistracted interaction. If you can only find fifteen minutes, take advantage of it. Fifteen minutes a day to connect with your spouse will help cultivate intimacy for the next fifteen years of marriage.

A weekly date is a commitment to block out larger blocks of time to nurture intimacy. The daily connection is helpful, but that can turn into a dull routine of sharing upcoming plans and recent updates. The weekly date serves as a way to slow down and enjoy one another. Whether it is a great meal, an enjoyable movie, or an outside activity, find the time to date one another throughout your marriage. Dating your spouse doesn't have to be expensive, but it will prove to be rewarding. If children or responsibilities make this challenging, get innovative regarding how to reclaim some time for one another.

A yearly getaway seeks to plan a vacation to enjoy one another for an extended period. While this may be difficult to find, attempt to acquire at least a weekend of time with no one else other than your spouse. As you remove yourself from daily responsibilities, you will be able to enjoy one another but also deepen your connection. Sacrifice might be needed, but you don't have to break the bank. While the cost of having a marriage getaway might be expensive, it is more costly not to have one.

Plan for a daily connection, a weekly date, and a yearly getaway. If any or all of those three seem impossible to obtain, that reveals how great the need is for your marriage's sake. Your calendar didn't get in this mess overnight, and it won't be fixed overnight either. Use these three commitments as a goal to hit. Even if it takes time to arrive at this ideal, make these connections a priority.

What God has joined together, let no busyness separate.

17 - Let No Busyness Separate

READ: Ephesians 5:15-17

REFLECT: Are you using your time wisely? Are there any adjustments that you need to make to your personal or family's calendar?

RESPOND: What plans can you make for a daily connection, a weekly date, and a yearly getaway?

18
Let No Finances Separate

Mishandling money can rob you of marital maturity.

One of the most significant sources of conflict in marriage is finances. The issue is not contingent upon how much money is present in the bank account but what you do with that money. While being strapped financially is naturally stressful, oftentimes, the marriages that have the most stress regarding finances are the ones that have more of it. How could finances stress both poor and rich couples? Money must be evil in of itself then. Actually, money isn't the root of evil – it's the love of money that is the root of evil.

> *For the love of money is a root of all kinds of evils. It is through this craving that some have wandered away from the faith and pierced themselves with many pangs (1 Tim. 6:10).*

Money alters the way people think and act. People think, say, and do unexpected things when it comes to wealth. If you are not careful, monetary obsession can tarnish something so beautiful as your marriage. What happens if one spouse is a spender and the other is a saver? How do you reconcile the conflict if one is a spreadsheet-making organized financial planner and the other is a receipt-losing disordered financial budgeteer? Can common ground be found between a generous giver and a hard-fisted hoarder?

Dealing with finances as an individual is stressful, but as a couple, it can be volatile. Agreeing upon a financial system is essential, but the motivation must be addressed to find unity. The best systems in the world can't fix character issues.

Financial stress is not a cash issue but a heart issue.

Comparison leads to discontentment which leads to treachery. When you see the possessions of another, envy sets in and you begin to think, "It's not fair." You must finish that thought – it's not fair to compare.

Comparison leads to discontentment. After looking at what others have, you start to realize the emerging dismal state of what you have. What's remarkable is that you didn't even think that way until being exposed to someone else's stuff.

Many couples fall into comparison traps with those beside them but also those before them. Keeping up with the status quo in your friend group or neighborhood can cause you to commit many financial blunders. You can view one's possessions easily and be prone to envy, but you don't know how they got what they got and what type of stress they are under to keep it. Don't let what others own own you.

Some couples struggle with a comparison to the standard by which their parents raised them. If they grew up in a wealthy household and never went without one day in their lives, the expectation has been set. Anything less than a beautiful house, a fancy car, a fashionable wardrobe, an expensive hobby, and a guaranteed vacation simply is unacceptable. Newlyweds quickly realize that they can't maintain the standard as adults by which they benefited as children, and the letdown can cause them to make poor choices that cost them more than they can afford.

Once discontentment nestles into your heart, you can justify any treacherous means to acquire more money or possessions. To achieve that desired standard, anything can become ethically possible. You can rationalize lying and justify stealing when you have convinced yourself that you deserve more.

To address finances in your marriage, you must understand the concepts of stewardship, partnership, and sponsorship. Stewardship means you are watching over something that isn't yours. It is the foundational belief that you are a caretaker of everything that you have.

All of your finances, property, and possessions are possessions of God since he owns everything (Deut. 10:14; Ps. 89:11; 1 Cor. 10:26). Even your mental and physical ability aligned with your work opportunities are all gifts that you receive from the Lord (1 Cor. 4:7). Once you grasp this truth, you begin to realize that every financial issue is a faith issue.

Having a partnership means you approach finances as a single unit rather than separate entities. Many marriages promote insecurity, suspicion, and selfishness because of maintaining personal finances outside the jurisdiction of a spouse's awareness. Many couples have different checking accounts and manage their own discretionary money, but I want to share another principle with you – oneness.

We come into this world alone (Gen. 2:18), but marriage seeks to provide a helper (Gen. 2:18) with whom we achieve oneness (Gen. 2:24). What that means is I don't have my stuff, and she has her stuff in marriage. We have our stuff. When you divide bills, responsibilities, and leisure money between you, there are these significant areas that are removed from the light and put into the dark (Luke 8:17; 1 Cor. 4:5). To have a genuine financial partnership, you must look at your resources together and seek to address the needs of your spouse as more important than your own needs (Phil. 2:4).

Sponsorship means that you view finances as a tool to impact others. Since we brought nothing into this world, we have to remind ourselves regularly that we cannot take anything out of it either (1 Tim. 6:7). With that in mind, how is your marriage investing financially for the glory of God and the good of others? Are you using God's resources for God's work?

If you belong to a local church, start by giving at least ten percent of your income to the work of the ministry. Tithing is a starting line of giving as it is an Old Testament principle now coupled with a New Testament generosity. From that point, figure out how you can support the church more or give to other worthwhile charities. As your compensation goes up, let your sponsorship go up with it. Find financial unity in sacrificial generosity.

What God has joined together, let no finances separate.

18 - Let No Finances Separate

READ: 1 Timothy 6:6-10

REFLECT: What is causing you the highest levels of discontent in your life right now?

RESPOND: What are some tangible adjustments you can make to have financial transparency and unity in your marriage?

19
Let No Hobby Separate

You don't have to be reminded to prioritize what you treasure.

We make space for what we love the most. No one has to convince us to take time for the things we love to do. We will even forsake rest and relaxation for the simple opportunity to continue with a hobby we adore. Jesus taught that "where your treasure is, there will your heart be also" (Luke 12:34). What we talk about most and what we spend the most time on often reveals what we treasure the greatest.

Regardless of how organized or unorganized you might claim to be, every person struggles with specific tasks and gravitates towards others. Unfortunately, we must often be reminded regarding the importance of maintaining spiritual disciplines to grow closer to the Lord. We all have those laborious tasks at work that we must be strongly encouraged to complete. Many of us fail to prioritize our marriages until we are coaxed, urged, or guilted. And yet, many of us have at least one activity that requires no reminders.

We each have that particular thing that relentlessly captures our attention and affections. Our hobbies can easily become our obsessions when we spend more thoughts, time, effort, and money on them than anything else. You know what it is, and so does everyone else around you.

Having a hobby is not necessarily an evil thing. If remaining in its proper place, a hobby can be a beneficial investment for you. Many of us need to engage in some regular activities that help us change up our daily schedule and marvel at God's gifts. If used correctly, an enjoyable hobby can cause us to glorify God and enjoy all of his good gifts (James 1:17).

Beware that there is always an outlying danger even for the most unsuspecting ideas or activities. Some hobbies are evil simply due to the nature of the activity. For the disciple of Jesus, some hobbies should be avoided due to their propensity to encourage sinful behaviors and to associate with depraved thinking (Eph. 4:17). Other hobbies can become evil due to the nature of our obsession with the activity. Not sinful in of itself, an enjoyable hobby can still cause a well-meaning person to neglect essential priorities for the believer.

A good thing can become a bad thing when it becomes the one thing to the neglect of the essential things.

It's all about balance. If you fail to achieve parity with nurturing family life and enjoying a healthy hobby, then a good thing becomes a bad thing. When driven to excess, a hobby that should help establish a healthier you does the exact opposite. Even if a hobby is a good thing, your family will learn to resent it if it takes time and affection away from them.

Your spouse will despise "the better you" if he or she isn't able to be around "the better you" as often. Once we invest time or resources into something, we can't use them on another. There's only so much to go around.

Working out can move from glorifying God by keeping our bodily temples healthy to glorifying ourselves by obsessing about our physical progress. Your spouse will probably desire the five-pound heavier you in the house than the five-pound lighter you in the gym. Any activity that always takes Saturdays away from your spouse limits your emotional intimacy since your day off from work turns into another day apart from each other.

Vehemently protecting time in a particular leisure activity while neglecting time to date your spouse rapidly dilutes a marriage. I have counseled many couples who are near divorce due to one spouse's downright obsession with a hobby. Your spouse can begin to despise the hobby which he or she initially encouraged as a healthy outlet for you. The other spouse felt jealous of the hobby and untrusting of the friends associated with the hobby.

You or your spouse's hobby can hurt your marriage, but so can your child's. Many parents turn into a chauffeur service shuttling their children to and fro from every hobby imaginable. Oftentimes, these hobbies will take the individuals away from opportunities to be the church, the family away from pivotal and limited time together, and the spouses away from time to connect.

Is the hobby that has your family running ragged going to pay the dividends back of what it costs you now? If they don't get the scholarship, make the team, or turn the hobby into a profession, was it worth these temporal commitments to disconnect from forever relationships? It might not be worth the significant investment.

In your marriage, you need a balance regarding your hobbies. Love your spouse and like your hobbies. If you begin to love these temporal hobbies more than your God-honoring commitments, you might run the risk of idolatry.

> *For all that is in the world – the desires of the flesh and the desires of the eyes and pride of life – is not from the Father but is from the world (1 John 2:16).*

Your fleshly desires will rob you of spiritual pursuits. If your hobby has no eternal weight to it, don't waste the majority of your hours of this temporal life upon it. Learn to seek contentment with the good things on earth (1 Tim. 6:6) while prioritizing to seek the godly things above (Col. 3:2; Matt. 6:33). Don't conform to this culture (Rom. 12:2) by obsessing over your hobbies in an unhealthy manner.

As a couple, seek agreement on what is healthy and appropriate for one's personal enjoyment as well as for the marriage's overall well-being. Be ready to explain your passions fully without exaggerating and be willing to listen to your spouse's desires without responding in a belittling or begrudging way. The quickest way to infuriate your spouse is to discredit something for which he or she genuinely loves. Agree upon reasonable and wise actions in order to prioritize that which deserves prioritizing.

What God has joined together, let no hobby separate.

19 - Let No Hobby Separate

READ: 1 John 2:15-17

REFLECT: How can the things of this world take you away from the will of God?

RESPOND: Ask your spouse if any of your hobbies are hindering the marriage. Be willing to make significant adjustments.

20

Let No Fox Separate

Sometimes the smallest things in marriage can become the most dangerous.

King Solomon recorded an excellent depiction of passionate, expectant love in the Song of Solomon. Known as the wisest man in all the earth (1 Kings 4:30; 10:23), he anticipated his wedding day by lavishing praise upon his ravishing bride. Taken aback by his unashamed love, she too publicly proclaimed her endearing affection for him. This type of love should have been able to handle any challenge that opposed them.

As they go back and forth, heaping complimentary praises towards one another, Solomon abruptly changes the vibe by instructing her with an unexpected exhortation:

> *"Catch the foxes for us, the little foxes, that spoil the vineyards, for our vineyards are in blossom" (SS 2:15).*

In the middle of this epic love poem, why does he bring up tiny foxes? Talk about killing the mood! In my experience, I can't imagine successfully wooing my woman by convincing her to hunt a varmint for me.

An understanding of the context will help unpack the biblical meaning. In Solomon's context, foxes would often come into a vineyard under the guise of darkness or stealthiness to spoil the harvest. Looking for an easy meal, they wouldn't consider why they should abstain from tampering with the produce. In a short amount of time, these animals could do significant damage before someone discovered them. Foxes weren't dangerous predators as much as they were annoying nuisances. If this couple failed to catch these pesky intruders, they wouldn't enjoy all the fruit that their vineyard should produce for them.

Every person needs to be aware of the little foxes scampering around his or her marriage. All marriages have specific minor issues that will turn into major issues if the couple refuses to address them. While there are definite marital predators out there, sometimes relationships struggle from the tiniest of annoyances that turn into the greatest of challenges.

Sometimes the most dangerous nuisances in your marriage are not the ones that are glaringly obvious.

They may be the simple, seemingly insignificant things that, if they remain unchecked, will ruin your marriage. In reality, these foxes might not even be sinful in of themselves, but they are nonetheless dangerous. Just as Solomon urged his bride to search, identify, and capture any fox loose in their marriage, we need to do the same. Are you aware of the most dangerous nuisances present in your marriage now?

These foxes run loose in every home. Have you ever had that marital disagreement that got heated but you couldn't remember what started it? You can probably recall that you disagreed with your spouse recently but unsure about the actual reason for the disagreement. I've helped couples who were so frustrated yet felt embarrassed to verbalize the point of their contention with one another. As a counselor, I have had to say sometimes, "No, refusing to wash the dishes is not a divorce-able offense." That issue wasn't that big of a problem until it remained unaddressed over time. Something that was small felt big because they never addressed it.

Any attempt to remove hindrances from your life is a stand for your marriage. The simple quest to identify them and the basic efforts to remove them show that you want your marriage to endure. Even while these foxes may seem small, they intend to ruin the vineyard.

In those times, the vineyard represented a source of blessing. It was a source of nourishment and income for a family unit as well as beneficial to the community around them. As these pestering foxes sought to benefit themselves, they were ruining the produce for those to whom it was intended and for those who could have benefited by mere association.

As your marriage endures challenges towards fruitfulness, realize that your marriage has an enemy and it isn't your spouse. A battle does exist for your marriage, but you need to remember whose side you are on. It is so easy to fight through challenges and somehow see your spouse as the antagonist.

You must resist any perspective that causes you to go to battle *against* your spouse when you should be going to battle *with* your spouse.

You should unite to combat the shared enemy. The foxes aren't trying to pick off the farmers; they are trying to take away that which is mutually beneficial to the farmers. They were attacking that which united and furthered them.

Why did Solomon want to catch the foxes? Their vineyards were in blossom, and they didn't want them ruined. They were producing. Their marriage was supposed to be vibrantly beneficial. Marriage was promised to be fruitful. All signs were in the positive, and he desperately wanted to keep it that way.

Realize that your marriage should be progressing towards greater intimacy and not drifting towards relational complacency. No matter how long you have been married, you should be experiencing blossoming growth. You should experience steady progress. If you aren't experiencing improvement in your marriage, it might be because you are allowing little foxes to run free through your home.

Where do you start? Look for the pesky intruders that seem to rob your marriage of what it should be. Commit to search, identify, and capture any small fox loose in your marriage. Look for the tiny nuisances that could cause great calamity if allowed to run free.

What God has joined together, let no fox separate.

20 - Let No Fox Separate

READ: Song of Solomon 2:10-17

REFLECT: What are some of the most common "foxes" that are ruining marriages today?

RESPOND: To which ones are your marriage most susceptible?

21

Let No Addiction Separate

Your marriage cannot survive the presence of any controlling factor other than the Holy Spirit.

Addiction can take many forms, and each type of addiction can cause different kinds of consequences. You can be addicted to alcohol, tobacco, illegal drugs, prescription drugs, gambling, food, social media, video games, cutting, shopping, and so much more. Some of the items on this list are dangerous due to sheer exposure, and some are dangerous when there is unbridled excess. The Apostle Paul clearly warned that believers should "not get drunk with wine, for that is debauchery, but be filled with the Spirit" (Eph. 5:18).

> **If something influences, alters, or controls your actions, the reality is that the Holy Spirit is no longer fully guiding you.**

Don't be led by spirits, but be led by the Spirit. While drunkenness is the sin he mentions in this context, the implication for any addictive activities is clear: don't be mastered by anything (1 Cor. 6:12). We can become addicted by being mastered by anything that completely garners our attention and affections. If the Bible portrays wine as something that causes mocking, fighting, and unwise behavior (Prov. 20:1), it is apparent that certain substances and activities cause us to act in a way that is uncharacteristic for God's children. We must resist anything that causes us not to behave like who we are called to be (Eph. 4:1).

It is heartbreaking to walk alongside someone who finally realizes that the cost of an addiction is a family. One such man came to our church during his time in rehab. Addiction had brought him to the absolute bottom. Finally clean, sober, and clear-headed, he was ready to make some changes. Within the safe walls of the center and the church, he was progressing well. The only hiccup in his discipleship was wrestling with why God wouldn't give him his family back. He had hurt them so many times and burned so many bridges; they had eventually thrown in the towel. While God's grace was readily available, his family's had run out. God would still use him, but he had to learn the awful truth about consequences - they don't depart with the addiction.

To the one who is addicted, stop denying your addiction. The addicted rarely acknowledges the problem, but those around him or her can see it clearly. If your spouse thinks there is a problem, you should at least heed the possibility. The very fact that your spouse is willing to bring up such a potentially volatile claim reveals that something isn't the way it should be. No one would want to go down this road unless there indeed is an issue that you need to address. Those without addiction problems don't have people approaching them with the suggestion of an addiction's presence. If your spouse brings it to your attention, you need to evaluate the claim earnestly.

Addiction has a scale. Maybe you aren't a "10" on a 10-point-scale, but your behavior is significant enough that your spouse has endangered peace in the house by talking about it. Even if you aren't a "10," a "5" needs to be addressed if it is hurting your marriage.

If you truly love your spouse, you will be willing to evaluate his or her accusation regarding your addictive behaviors. Love your spouse more than the object of your fascination and consider a change. Professing love is easy, but proving love is difficult.

> *Many a man proclaims his own steadfast love,*
> *but a faithful man who can find (Prov. 20:6)?*

Faithfulness proves itself. It's one thing to say you love your spouse, but it's another thing to demonstrate it. Mere verbal acknowledgment is simply insufficient. Stop denying you have a problem if the person who loves you most says there is one. Be willing to seek out legitimate and godly help to make a change.

To the one who loves the addicted one, stop enabling his or her addiction. Addiction doesn't get better by itself. A person struggling with addiction minimizes life by centering life around the object of the habit. Even if you desire to keep your spouse happy, to allow addictive behaviors to continue without challenge is a detriment to him or her. Neglecting to address severe issues is not love.

Getting involved in a confrontation is incredibly messy, but continuing to enable the behavior will be even messier. You must love your spouse more than you love his or her happiness. Some label addiction as a sickness, but it is at least a sickness birthed and sustained within a sinful person. You cannot allow sin to go unchecked with your spouse. Confront sin where you see it out of love for your spouse (1 Pet. 4:8; James 5:19-20).

To both parties in a marriage with a person struggling with addiction, stop distancing yourself from the relationships you need the most: God, one another, and some godly support. Shame frequently causes us to cover up and hide our issues rather than offering humble acknowledgment for the sake of deliverance.

Don't distance yourself from God. Come together in prayer asking for his divine intervention to combat such a significant stronghold (2 Cor. 10:4). Fill your heart and mind with the truths of Scripture that can help you fight off the enemy's influence (Eph. 6:17). Submit yourself to God's design for your life and resist the devil's schemes to watch him flee (James 4:7).

Don't distance yourself from one another. Learn how to fight with each other instead of against each other. Continual frustration and recurring disappointment can cause you to separate you from your spouse during this time. If your marriage can emerge from addiction victorious, you will have to learn how to bear with one another's sins patiently (Col. 3:13).

Don't distance yourself from godly support. Your church is not a museum of perfect people but a hospital for sick people (Mark 2:17). You are not alone. Be honest with your pastor and close, godly friends who can walk with you during this time.

What God has joined together, let no addiction separate.

21 - Let No Addiction Separate

READ: Proverbs 23:29-35

REFLECT: What addictions could most easily separate your marriage?

RESPOND: Ask your spouse if he or she sees any addictive behavior present in your life and humbly consider the answer. Determine the next step to address any current concern.

22

Let No Adultery Separate

Marriage cannot work with three people in it.

While that may seem like common sense thinking, it apparently is not. Many marriages end due to an adulterous relationship when one makes allowance for another person to engage in privileges that should be reserved solely for a spouse. One of the first commandments given to God's people to distinguish them from the godless culture around them dealt with marriage and adultery.

You shall not commit adultery (Ex. 20:14).

A common misconception of adultery is that it starts as a physical rendezvous. While that can happen, it usually occurs much more subtly. As Christians, we have a real enemy. Satan is trying to destroy your family right now (1 Pet. 5:8). You may not be completely aware of his ploys, but he has already set things in motion to take down your marriage and to devastate your children. He has enlisted help through the efforts of selfish, seductive flirts and unfaithful, unresolved spouses, but he loves to use any props necessary to destroy a marriage.

One of his greatest tactics against marriages is his fantasy-type portrayal of adultery. The adventure of seduction awakens many bored spouses. The danger of it all provides an excitement that may have been lacking for some time.

Satan is very good at allowing people to see the benefits of an affair while hiding the consequences. He helps them imagine sex with the other person. He provides opportunities to develop an emotional connection. Conveniently, he neglects to reveal the lifetime of pain for mere passing moments of pleasure.

The fun of adultery will last for a moment, but the pain of adultery will last for a lifetime.

You may think that the person flirting with you wants your body, mind, or companionship, but Scripture says that the person enticing you to commit adultery wants to take your very life (Prov. 6:26). People don't usually see the person with whom they are having a fling as desiring to ruin their lives. Most likely, the person with whom the affair is happening with seems to care for that person genuinely. Make no mistake about it, the flirt might have flattering intentions, but he or she is enticing you to make decisions that will forever devastate your life. You may find gracious reconciliation after an affair, but your life will never be the same after it.

If you play with fire, you are going to get burned (Prov. 6:27). God is clear that anyone who sleeps with another man's wife will be punished (Prov. 6:29; Heb. 13:4), and his lack of discipline (Prov. 5:20-23) and sense in this matter will destroy himself (Prov. 6:32). Such actions as adultery are so vile that they don't belong among those citizens of the Kingdom (Eph. 5:5).

God commanding something should serve as sufficient reasoning to abstain, but if you need additional logic, realize that adultery will impact every single area of your life. While a romantic encounter is pleasurable, is it worth making your children have two birthday parties each year because you and your former spouse can't be in the same room? Are you willing to lose all common friends and watch them turn against you in defense of your spouse? Is adultery worth losing all that you have built with your spouse - spiritually, emotionally, and even financially?

When adultery has taken root, you no longer think of those consequences because you believe your love will be sufficient. In adultery, you can never be in love but only in lust. The old preacher-ism applies to adultery so well: Sin will take you farther than you want to go, keep you longer than you want to stay, and cost you more than you want to pay.

The irony of adultery is that as soon as you get the person your pursued, he or she ceases to be the person you admired.

Adultery changes a person. Committing this transgression alters a person in significant ways. Do you admire him as a dad? If he has an affair with you, he is now a shameful father who has broken the heart of his family and painfully betrayed the mother of those precious children. Do you admire her as a caring person? She's not caring if she is willing to have an affair with you and destroy those who love you the most. As soon as you sink your claws into that person, he or she is no longer the type of person you want anymore. How can you even start a relationship with someone you can't trust? How can you ensure that you won't do this to one another in a few years from now?

There are a few textbook scenarios that usually start affairs. When a need goes unmet, someone goes looking. When a disconnection widens, a person puts out feelers. When discontentment grows, a desperate person resorts to desperate measures.

Adultery doesn't start in the bed; it begins in the heart. Jesus said that infidelity starts with lusting after someone in your heart (Matt. 5:28). Is there someone with whom you can picture yourself? Any fantasies that linger in your mind? Are you comparing your spouse with someone else? Be very careful.

If you are currently in an affair or dangerously close to it, there is only one solution: coldly drop that person and never speak to him or her again. If that seems harsh, let me remind you that it is not nearly as severe as what you have already done to your spouse with that person. Your fling is not your responsibility. Your spouse is your priority. Your marriage is God-ordained, and your affair was satanically organized. While physical connections, emotional weight, and relational dependence has unfortunately been created through this affair, you have to end it now and stop concerning yourself with that person's well-being. You have another person's well-being to worry about – the one whom you promised to God that you would be faithful to until the end.

What God has joined together, let no adultery separate.

22 - Let No Adultery Separate

READ: Proverbs 7:1-27

REFLECT: What are some ways that you can affair-proof your marriage?

RESPOND: Can you identify a flirt or acknowledge an attraction in your heart for a specific person? You need to cut off ties altogether. Be blunt and cold, and get yourself as far from fire as fast as you can.

23
Let No Pornography Separate

Pornography seeks to convince you that what is God-given is insufficient to meet your desires.

A marriage cannot experience intimacy when more than two people exist within the relationship. The marriage bed is often overcrowded due to how one or both partners have consumed pornography and altered the concept of reality regarding sex. This voyeuristic pandemic is robbing couples of marital oneness and sexual enjoyment.

You must ruthlessly combat pornography because it is a vile attack on marriage. It seeks to invade the precious marital union with images, videos, and ideas designed to belittle your spouse's worth and to endanger your marriage's commitment. Since marriage is something that God puts together, it should remain in a rightful standing of honor and purity before God and protected from any open invitation or contaminated intrusion.

> *Marriage should be honored by all, at the marriage bed kept pure, for God will judge the adulterer and the sexually immoral (Heb. 13:4).*

To honor your marriage, you must keep the marriage bed pure from anyone else invading it. That includes real experiences and virtual experiences. Sex isn't the problem. Sexual desires are not the issue. The dilemma is when we attempt to meet a God-given desire in an ungodly way. You are supposed to have your sexual needs with your spouse and pornography is robbing you both.

Pornography is a cheap, quick, sinful, and pathetic attempt to fulfill a God-given desire.

The husband who asked to meet with me was in trouble. His wife had found pornography on his computer, and he understood why she was upset but couldn't comprehend why she was *that* upset. In his mind, his sin was unfortunate, but she should be relieved that he had not committed an "actual affair." As someone who had saved her body for him, worked out in the gym to keep it in shape for him, and regularly prioritized intimacy with him, she interpreted his problem as her problem. What was wrong with *her* that he needed to go to *that*? His selfishness led to her insecurity. In her mind, he had cheated on her repeatedly. The thought of sex repulsed her because she no longer felt it was something special between them. One moment of what seemed like harmless pornography turned into years of dealing with the consequences of bitterness and distrust.

When the concept of pornography comes up, most people's minds drift towards media content containing a significant level of debauchery. The blatant pornographic material in print, videos, and web content must be addressed, but beware of compartmentalizing pornography. Lustfully gazing at someone who is not your spouse can turn into an obsessive consumption of pornographic material, and both of them are sinful. Years ago, someone had to work hard to obtain such pornographic content, but nowadays the content comes looking for you. It's no longer difficult to find porn, it's difficult to avoid it.

Since men seem to struggle with sexual sins more, we tend to believe that women don't battle in this arena and that premise is simply untrue. Women are in danger just as much as men are. What is dangerous is that a man's pornographic tendencies are often overt and rightfully viewed as disgusting and vile, but a woman's identical actions are casually regarded as harmless and fun.

For women, they must be careful because they don't usually see their lighthearted actions, casual comments, and media consumption as sinful. Be cautious that your commitment to the reality show, your following of a favorite actor, or your obsession with that certain musician is not actually immoral. We berate men in society for their sex-saturated brains and women are often given a free pass to indulge.

All lust is sinful. We need consistent standards. Pornography is printed or visual material that is intended to stimulate erotic feelings, and it can invade your marriage in many ways. No chiseled body of your spouse can ever fully compete with the guise of photoshopped celebrities. Any exposure to scripted sexual acts analyzes your marriage sexual intimacy into an unrealistic comparison trap. Being quasi-fulfilled sexually through pornography reduces your efforts to pursue your spouse romantically. Satan is using our culture to invade your marriage bed and to tell you that your spouse isn't enough. He is a vile liar (John 8:44) who is trying to devour you (1 Pet. 5:8).

At some level, every marriage has been affected by sought-out or stumbled-upon pornography. You are not alone. Even while the time is different, lustful thoughts were a problem even when the Bible was written.

Job made a covenant with his eyes about not looking at another woman (Job 31:1). Solomon warned his son not to be captured by the beautiful appearance of another woman (Prov. 6:25). Paul taught that God's will for all believers was their sanctification which meant abstaining from sexual immorality (1 Thess. 4:3). He urged that not even a hint of it should be found in our lives (Eph. 5:3). Jesus even taught that adultery honestly started in the heart when someone looked lustfully at another (Matt. 5:27-28).

If you want to protect your marriage bed, you have to kick out every fantasy that has invaded it.

Jesus was clear. If your eyes cause you to stumble, you should tear them out (Matt. 18:9). Besides physical mutilation, how do we apply this command? Get rid of any technological devices that give you sinful opportunities. Put on blocks. Install passwords that only your spouse knows how to unlock. Add filters. Get an accountability partner. Do whatever it takes.

Your spouse deserves your best, and you will give that when you still believe he or she is the best. Stop looking at someone that doesn't belong to you. Chase pornography out of your life before its consumption drives you out of your home.

What God has joined together, let no pornography separate.

23- Let No Pornography Separate

READ: Matthew 5:27-30

REFLECT: Why would Jesus equate adultery of the heart as serious as adultery of the body?

RESPOND: Is pornography affecting your marriage? How will you fight against it today?

24
Let No Technology Separate

Without moderation, technology will distract and disconnect you from your spouse.

With the ever-growing rise of technology, we are more connected and yet more disconnected than ever before. In one way, we are more connected with distant acquaintances than we were previously through a level of pseudo-community that social media and technology provides through recent updates and constant information. In another way, we are more disconnected from the people who are physically around us due to the constant barrage of interruptions and distractions. The shift has made it easier for us to talk through devices than to talk in person nowadays.

Technology causes us to seek limited community in digital spaces and forsake authentic relationships in physical places. The type of digital opportunities that can distract us seem unlimited. The rapid development of technology ensures that by the time I highlight a list of current technological trends, it will be obsolete and dated by the time you read it.

One thing is for sure – the options aren't slowing down. Adults who used to be concerned over the next generation's over-usage of the living room television or the landline telephone couldn't have even fathomed the dramatic rise of media mediums. While the actual list will continually change, the categories of our digital obsessions are standard: devices (the mediums we plug into the wall), applications (the functions we use), and content (the programs and persons with which we interact on the devices). In those three categories, we have numerous options of possibilities to distract us from what matters most in our lives.

The fact is that technology is not evil in of itself. Technology is amoral – it is without morals. An amoral hammer can be used to build a house or break a finger; the power lies in how one wields it. The function is more important than the form. Amoral agents can be used for good or evil.

Without a doubt, technology provides an opportunity to encourage your spouse during the day, connect with relationships far away, glean insight from wisdom in distant places, share truth on numerous platforms, and increase productivity for the benefit of others. Those are all very beneficial uses. But despite those blessings, an amoral technological device can turn into an unhealthy distraction. How are we supposed to determine what amount of technology usage is useful and what is dangerous?

> *"All things are lawful for me," but not all things are helpful.*
> *"All things are lawful for me," but I will not be enslaved*
> *by anything (1 Cor. 6:12).*

The Apostle Paul warned that lawful things could become unlawful things when they enslave us. Not everything that is acceptable is helpful. In a passage focused on the dangers of immorality, he warned the church to beware of the power of alluring unrighteous behavior.

In the sinful list he included (1 Cor. 6:9-10), some of those sins are inappropriate ways to obtain appropriate desires. Sex isn't evil, but sexual immorality is. Money isn't evil, but greed is. He understood that when a desire enslaves us, sin will be rampant. Even if some things are lawful and acceptable for us, the moment that it masters us, those good things have now become evil things that we must quickly address.

Master technology so that it doesn't master you. Use it until it starts using you. If you prioritize a device more than a relationship, you must war against that tendency. If you aren't careful, technology will tempt you to neglect your marriage relationship. Satan arrived on the pages of Scripture once God instituted marriage, and his temptation brought about sin that ultimately caused them to hide from God and distance themselves from one another. Since technology has the potential to distance yourself from God and your spouse, you must be on guard against its subtle luring.

The litmus test of technology is simple: is your usage of technology helping your marriage or hurting your marriage?

To combat technological distractions separating your marriage, review these considerations. First, evaluate your personal usage of digital media. What devices or content seem to have a hold on you? Install a block or a tracker to see how much time you spend on the devices. Be willing to make adjustments. You might be shocked to see how much time you actually invest into digesting digital content. Don't say that you don't have time for your family if you make time for your media.

Second, share experiences with your spouse. Many marriages would dramatically improve if they would take their eyes off the devices and adjust their eyes towards each other. You might be shocked at how much better your marriage could be if you put your hands on your spouse more than you put your hands on your device. I can't make it any plainer than that - spend time enjoying all the components of your marriage. The real person beside you is far better than any content you could download. Don't warm yourself behind the glow of individual screens. Agree on how and when you will utilize technology in your home, and commit that if you are going to partake of media, at least make time to engage with it together.

Third, be careful of pointing out your spouse's technological obsessions while refusing to address your own. If your spouse points out an annoyance with your media consumption, listen to what he or she is saying and don't revert to a juvenile justification of your usage based upon his or her usage. Take the digital log out of your eye before you attempt to remove the technological speck from your spouse's eye (Matt. 7:5). What are you willing to change for the sake of your marriage?

What God has joined together, let no technology separate.

24 - Let No Technology Separate

READ: 1 Corinthians 6:12-20

REFLECT: How is technology helping your marriage? How is it hurting your marriage?

RESPOND: Resolve that all technology devices be put away every day until you have connected conversationally and physically to some degree. Eliminate any concerns your spouse has.

25
Let No Password Separate

In a time of increased connectivity with others, you must learn how to maintain transparency with your spouse.

With the ever-increasing rise of social media and the barrage of technological interaction, marriages can become endangered if you do not put proper precautions in place. Operating from numerous devices and connecting through various mediums, we can communicate with people in a host of ways more than ever before. The ability to privately connect with people on numerous platforms is at an unprecedented level and will continue to increase. The media tide will not wane, so how will you prepare to meet its challenges and demands?

Through numerous technological inboxes, we position ourselves to meet, dialogue, interact, share, and reconnect with all types of people. Whether they are present acquaintances or past relationships, the ability to connect is conveniently placed at our fingertips. While these digital tools in of themselves are not evil, they can lead to corrupt practices that can harm your marriage by fostering isolation and a private section of your life. Do you see the danger?

The easiest way to protect your marriage in an online world is to share your passwords with your spouse. If you immediately feel defensive to such a concept, you might be in more danger than you realize. While living in a secretive, individualistic society, you must resist the trend towards isolation and commit to complete transparency within your marriage.

God never described marriage as two individuals living as roommates while maintaining private lives. The oneness present in marriage (Gen. 2:24) should spill over into every arena of who we are. Committing to someone via marriage forever exposed all of the potential hiding places to which we could run.

But if we walk in the light, as he is in the light, we have fellowship with one another, and the blood of Jesus his Son cleanses us from all sin (1 John 1:7).

Walking in the light is characterized by a lifestyle that isn't seeking to hide something from God and others. When Jesus cleanses us, it allows us to have a transparent walk before him and also have close fellowship with one another. Jesus has promised that everything that we do in the dark he will eventually bring to the light (Luke 8:17). So, if there is a secret life going on behind technological doors, it will be uncovered one day. If you make yourself willingly transparent to your spouse, you are creating trust in your marriage and diminishing the opportunity to walk outside the lines.

I usually don't return a missed call from an unfamiliar number. A college student once told me that she had called my phone but didn't leave a message. When she saw me later, she asked if my wife had a cell phone since I mentioned both of our names on my voicemail. When I told her that we both had cell phones and both of our voicemails said the same thing, she replied, "So do you do that so that girls like me know that your wife could check your phone or voicemail at any time?" I was thankful that she received that not-so-subtle hint. Just the awareness of our open policies with one another spoke volumes to another.

Sharing your password with your spouse willingly provides unhindered access to your media activity. If you feel like such a move creates distrust in a marriage, I want to propose that it might build even more trust between the two of you. By such a move, you aren't preemptively accusing your spouse but proactively trusting your spouse. When you put up boundaries, you are simply understanding the dangers out there and want to give each other the best chance to succeed.

You may trust the person but not trust the environment.

Encouraging a recovering alcoholic to avoid hanging out in a bar is not distrust – it's pure wisdom. Locking your doors when an escaped convict is dangerously on the loose is not judgmental spite but cautious concern. Picking up a fearful child when a stray dog runs up is not restrictive but protective. So when you open yourself up to your spouse to maintain integrity for what you might do or what someone might try to do to you, you are showing trust in the person but not in the environment.

Transparency can't prevent sin, but it can protect from sin.

If you want to sin, you will find a way to sin. No amount of barriers can stop a rebellious will. Sinful people will always make a way to do what they want to do. But when you take a measure like sharing your password with your spouse, you are putting up another hedge of protection (Job 1:8; Eph. 6:13).

Marriage deserves complete honesty and absolute transparency. There should be no more thought of a mine versus yours mentality in this relationship. You have nothing to which your spouse shouldn't have access. As one, there should be no area that is off-limits to your spouse.

Among counseling needs within a church, I have always been an advocate for installing windows in places where we needed to close doors. It is critical to flee even the appearance of evil (1 Thess. 5:22). In one situation, as we installed doors in the pastoral offices, someone inquired if there was a situation we were addressing. I responded that we didn't have a problem, and we wanted to keep it that way.

By providing your spouse to have free range through your life, you are creating an open-door policy for your marriage. Since you will have to interact with other people in your life who are not your spouse, take precautions to develop trust in your relationship. Where you need to close a door, you need to cut out a hole for a window. To obtain candid confidence, provide your passwords to every device and platform you have. Feel free to share your stance with others to broadcast to the masses that they don't have a chance to separate your marriage. What you have is too precious.

What God has joined together, let no password separate.

25 - Let No Password Separate

READ: 1 John 1:5-10

REFLECT: How does living in the dark hinder true fellowship with your spouse?

RESPOND: What areas do you need to cut a hole for a window? How will you share your passwords with your spouse?

26

Let No Midlife Crisis Separate

It's more important how your marriage finishes than how it began.

Even if your wedding day had drama surrounding it, most would view that event as a joyful and hopeful time. The early days are supposed to be comfortable and carefree. We usually classify overly positive married folk as those who are still "honeymooning" as an implication that marriage is simple in the beginning and yet difficult later. As you age, life provides many joys, but it also supplies numerous frustrations. Each spouse will go through significant slumps without warning or welcoming during various seasons of life. Don't wonder if it will happen but determine how you will handle it when those seasons come your way.

Even though the term "midlife crisis" has only been used in recent decades, the cultural phenomenon is significant in its apparent impact. Usually described to happen between the ages of 35 to 60, people reach a critical juncture where they experience different levels of disappointment regarding one's life. A person reaches midlife, looks around at his or her body, family, career, home, and wealth to inquire this penetrating question: "Is this it?"

Not only do you feel defeated by comparing your situation to what others have, but you also compare yourself to what you thought you would have or what you should have. As youthfulness distances itself in the rearview mirror, aches and pains increase daily, glory days are nothing but a farfetched memory, and unmet expectations run rampant through one's mind, it can lead a person into a severe state of depression, reevaluation, or rebellion.

Stereotypically, people assume someone is struggling through a midlife crisis when a flashy new vehicle is purchased, a toned body is desired, or an exciting hobby is pursued. While these can be legitimate indications of such a crisis, the motivation behind the symptoms is the most critical piece to evaluate. What does he or she see as lacking and what level of desperation does he or she possess to ensure its possession?

In cases where I have seen a midlife crisis separate a marriage, the person changing makes sudden and significant adjustments in life. The people around the struggling individual will often comment, "What has gotten into him?" or "This isn't like her." If it seems like a drastic change, you would be correct. The individual has been awoken to his or her rapidly impending downward spiral of aging and is desperate to change something.

The only way to survive a midlife crisis is by focusing on what you have rather than what you don't have.

Your identity is in Christ and not in your accomplishments. Value the spouse that you have over the spouse you wish you had. If you could spare your soul from unrealistic and unhealthy expectations, you would realize that you are blessed beyond measure. If you know Christ, you truly are blessed with every spiritual blessing (Eph. 1:3) and every need is fulfilled (Phil. 4:19).

Every person will experience unexpected frustrations and debilitating disappointments. You and your spouse will struggle at different points in your life to varying degrees. Watching your spouse struggle will bring sorrow and stress to your own life. During those times, resist the urge to distance yourself from your partner. Too often do spouses kick one another while the other is down instead of offering a hand to help him or her up. Being married implies that your spouse should be in your corner there to help you up when you can no longer help yourself up (Ecc. 4:9-10).

If we each will experience this phenomenon of a midlife crisis to some varying extent, we must consider how to prepare for it, endure through it, and share after it. In your efforts to combat this dangerous time in your life, don't learn lessons that you fail to share with someone else. Regardless of how old you are, preparing for a midlife crisis starts today. Even though the best day to plant a tree was decades ago, the second best day is today. The same is accurate with spiritual slumps.

Even while you have hopefully been building endurance into your life for decades, if you haven't, don't neglect its importance another moment. Plant your entire life in the nurturing soil of God's Word by meditating on it day and night so that you will not fall during times of drought (Ps. 1:2-3). The more that you apply this Word into your life, the more successful you will become (Josh. 1:8). The delights and disciplines you put into your life now will emerge at the times when you need them most.

The Spirit will bring to your remembrance what you have deposited (John 14:26), so make sure you are digging deep, so he has plenty from which to draw. As you focus on your Creator in the days of your youth, you prepare yourself for the coming evil days that lack the previous pleasures (Ecc. 12:1).

However and whenever your struggles do hit, endure through them. Be honest with God and with your spouse about the state of your life. Discern what is accurate and what is amplified due to an invalid comparison and an ungodly culture. Surround yourself regularly with other believers who can spur you on to love and good deeds (Heb. 10:24-25). Make it through one day at a time.

And let steadfastness have its full effect, that you may be perfect and complete, lacking in nothing (James 1:4).

After you emerge from such a time of struggle, share your experiences after it. God uses these times to help you become steadfast. How could you watch a person enter into a storm that you just came out of without providing instructions on how to survive? Find those younger men and women in your life whom you can disciple and mentor through these challenging seasons. Proclaim God's goodness during the younger years and the later years (Ps. 71:17).

What God has joined together, let no midlife crisis separate.

26 - Let No Midlife Crisis Separate

READ: James 1:2-8

REFLECT: In what areas of your life are you currently in need of God's wisdom?

RESPOND: Would you be honest with God and your spouse regarding your evaluation of your life? What do you need to build into your life intentionally to combat possible slumps?

27
Let No Incompatibility Separate

Marital conflict does not imply that you are hopelessly incompatible but that you are relentlessly sinful.

At the beginning of your relationship, opposites attract, but as you continue together, opposites attack. Remember the time when your spouse's differences made him or her more attractive to you? As you started to date one another, you were drawn to what caused this object of your affection to be unique compared to others. Not only was his or her personality intriguing but you honestly felt as if this person's strengths complimented your weaknesses. Your incompatibility was a promising potential regarding the budding romance. This person was uniquely designed to complete what was lacking in you.

How did the alluring potential of two uniquely different people gradually turn into a war between an incompatible couple that now resorts to believing they should have never been paired together? Through the seasons of marriage, couples begin to experience moments in which they realize they are desperately out of sync with one another. Whether it comes in the area of social preferences, emotional needs, conversational patterns, sexual ideals, or spiritual convictions, couples find themselves at polarized odds with one another.

Many disillusioned couples will remark that their spouse changed through the years. How could you not change? Think about what life has dealt you, how age has paced you, and what circumstances have surprised you. Each of you has dramatically changed. If you are still trying to love the version of your spouse you met down the aisle of the church on your wedding day, you have fallen victim to a case of mistaken identity. The exact person you met at the marriage altar doesn't exist anymore. Your spouse has changed and will continue to change. The drastic perspective and persona shift makes many couples believe that they should have never gotten married in the first place. Once they arrive at that line of thinking, divorce is the logical option for many couples.

Divorce is not the solution. Divorce is the complete opposite of the only appropriate solution. If you feel as if your marriage is incompatible, the only workable solution is to continue long-term marital commitment. You can abandon the commitment to your spouse and run into the arms of another relationship that initially seems compatible, but time will reveal the same thing – you are not entirely compatible with anyone. In reality, that's the point of marriage. God is more interested in your marriage's commitment than in its compatibility.

Your marriage is not a contract where your commitment to your spouse is somehow conditional upon his or her behavior. Contracts are where one person lives by the mantra that if my spouse does *this*, then I will do *that*. Marriage covenants are a different agreement altogether. Where contracts are meant to keep you safe, covenants are intended to keep the other person safe. The marriage covenant implies that you will do what you are supposed to do regardless of the commitment of the other.

Even if your spouse decides to change for the worse, your biblical responsibility is to remain faithful to God and your spouse regardless. The Prophet Malachi spoke out against numerous injustices among God's people. One issue that notably provoked him was the lack of sincere followthrough among the people in the covenant of marriage.

> *...The LORD was witness between you and the wife of your youth, to whom you have been faithless, though she is your companion and your wife by covenant (Mal. 2:14).*

Isn't it interesting that the prophet includes the phrase "the wife of your youth?" He is emphasizing the need to prioritize the marriage vows in the later years while acknowledging that they were so much easier to maintain in the earlier days. The installment of this covenant keeps you diligently aware that your spouse is your companion. You have made a promise with him or her and to God. Marriage isn't something to discard lightly. The only reason the Scripture says you would throw in the towel on your marriage is not that you are unfaithful but because you are faithless. Do you lack faith that God can make your marriage work again? Believe that he is able!

The problem in your marriage is not that you are two different people but that you are two sinful people. If you think that claim seems too harsh of a postulation, you are failing to realize the trivial nature of your reasoning. You desire to discard a marital covenant over a temporary trait. Even if your differences aren't inherently sinful, your response to your spouse's differences is unabashedly corrupt. You believe that a divorce is a logical option for personal preferences. Would you honestly break a covenant before God because of petty differences?

You must value your commitment over your compatibility.

Acknowledging your differences, you put your inclinations to the side and value your spouse's desires more important than your own (Phil. 2:3-4). Even though each of you has annoying quirks, you must accept the truth that two are better than one (Ecc. 4:9). In marriage, you belong to one another.

Solomon's bride stated it succinctly, "I am my beloved's, and his desire is for me" (SS 7:10). She didn't say that their desires were the same. She just said that she belonged to him, and his passion was not like hers, but it actually was her! That's what every couple must resolve to do – base a marriage on a commitment to one another rather than the fleeting moments of compatibility.

Marriage is not when two people give fifty percent. Marriage is when two people both give one hundred percent. Don't wait for your spouse to fix his or her problems before repairing your own. Address the significant issues and overlook the quirks. Even if you feel increasingly incompatible, allow your commitment to one another to stand firm.

What God has joined together, let no incompatibility separate.

27 - Let No Incompatibility Separate

READ: Malachi 2:10-16

REFLECT: Would you want your child to be married to someone like yourself right now? Why or why not?

RESPOND: Commit to loving your spouse regardless of the present compatibility. Sort your issues out into what is significant and what is insignificant.

28
Let No Hardship Separate

The strongest couples are the ones who refuse to allow the hardships that come against their marriage to come in between their marriage.

What if there was a way to preview coming trials in a marriage on the wedding day? Before the couple vows to love one another "for better for worse," a news crew from the future would provide a teaser clip of what was yet to come in the subsequent decades of marriage. The joyous moment would instantly reek with somber gravity. Some might run from the altar in utter fear of the upcoming challenges! The reality is that none of our marriages ever saw the troubles coming. In naiveté, we committed that we would be with one another no matter what happened. We would survive it all. Regardless of what came our way, we would make it together.

Then "it" happened. That sickness was unexpected. That death was unwarned. The stress was too high. The provision was too low. The prodigal shouldn't have run off. The circumstance wasn't supposed to come near.

These unplanned trials never even asked our permission to interrupt our lives. Some of them were within our control, but many of them were not. The consequences of our hands and the circumstances of our lives leveled our stability and forever impacted our relationship with one another. Regardless of how long ago you said your vows to one another, your marriage has already endured numerous, unexpected trials, and in full disclosure, there are probably more to come. You can't protect your marriage from experiencing hardships, but you can prepare for them and persevere through them.

When hardships come, people often want to discover the source behind them. In this life, that information is often difficult to ascertain. Is God testing you? Is Satan tempting you? Are enemies trying you? Are consequences troubling you? In reality, you may never discover each hardship's origin.

> **You can waste every waking moment of your hurt trying to discover the reason when you should be focusing on your response.**

It is what it is. You cannot change what has happened in your life. There isn't a rewind button that will let you go backward. The only way to move forward is to address where you are right now and not where you wish you were. Regardless of the source of your hardship, the response to each situation is the same – remain faithful to God and your spouse. That's all you can do now. If God is testing, stay faithful. If Satan is tempting, stay faithful. If enemies are trying, stay faithful. If consequences are troubling, stay faithful. The presence of hardships is surer than the reasoning for them.

How can two different couples experience the same tragedy and handle it so differently? The tragic event that caused one couple to divorce caused the other couple to come out stronger on the other side. While there isn't a simple answer, I have realized something about couples whose marriages stay intact during hardships: they don't allow their own pain to blind them to their spouse's pain. Instead of attempting to heal in isolation, they try to bind up the wounds of their partner.

To stay faithful to God during hardships, allow the trial to bring you closer to God rather than further away. As you hold onto your Father in the waves, your grasp around his neck should be tighter the deeper that you go. If you have questions for him, don't be afraid to ask. He is big enough to handle it. When overwhelmed with sorrow, Job wanted answers (Job 23:17), David wanted nearness (Ps. 71:12), John the Baptist wanted clarity (Matt. 11:3), Paul wanted relief (2 Cor. 12:8), and even Jesus wanted assurance (Matt. 26:42). If you have ever desired any of these things, you are in some outstanding company. I honestly believe some hardships are graciously provided in our lives so that we are forced to draw nearer to the only source that can give comfort now and peace for that which is coming of which we are yet unaware.

To stay faithful to your spouse during hardships, remember that it is better to endure trials in cooperation *with* one another rather than in isolation *from* one another. Don't let sorrow, resentment, or frustration keep you from this gift of a person intended to be a God-given helper (Gen. 2:18). The waters designed to quiet your love are incapable of quenching your love (SS 8:7). Give allowance to one another to be in the pit but don't allow one another to stay there.

Your marriage might be going through one of the most challenging seasons right now that you have ever experienced together. It's almost as if you are in an intense battle and don't know how you are even going to survive. When I have watched epic battle sequences in movies, I always wonder how difficult it would be to maintain a sense of accuracy in the heat of the battle. As two armies run to the battle line, it is clear which solider is fighting for which battalion. But as the battle rages on, your frame of reference is continuously challenged.

I wonder how often someone backs into an unknown soldier and out of heightened defenses takes a swing without the time to see for which side the solider is fighting. As the body count rises, the only way to focus your bearings is to raise your gaze upwards and to run to your side. You look for your army's banner flying high above because you know it's a safe place to run. Maybe that's why Solomon's bride equated his love to a banner raised high above her.

> **He brought me to the banqueting house,**
> **and his banner over me was love (Song of Solomon 2:4).**

In the chaotic battle of this life, this bride understood that the safest place to go was under the love of her husband. As the war raged on, she knew where to run. His love was the grounding force. In times when it was difficult to see who was even on your side, she looked up to what made her confident. He took her to the banqueting house. When chaos surrounded her, she reoriented her perspective by going to the safest place she knew. Are you a safe banner for your spouse?

What God has joined together, let no hardship separate.

28 - Let No Hardship Separate

READ: Psalm 27:1-14

REFLECT: What hardship is your marriage currently experiencing?

RESPOND: How can you draw closer to God and your spouse?

29
Let No Spiritual Apathy Separate

The best way to nurture both the relationship with your God and your spouse is if they are in proximity with one another.

When you got married, you received a built-in accountability partner. With a spouse, God provides a great gift to help with your sanctification. As you seek to mature completely in Christ (Col. 1:29), here is a person that can help you regularly if you will let him or her.

I can remember being convicted by my wife on Saturdays early on in our marriage. She wasn't trying to be my Holy Spirit, but the Holy Spirit was definitely using her. As I would eagerly prioritize leisurely activities, I would often go searching to see what my bride was doing in the house.

Frequently, I would stumble upon her beside that huge window in that blue room with her Bible open. As soon as we made eye contact, I would try to make up some bogus explanation of why I hadn't spent time with the Lord yet that morning and that my next intention was to do just that. As I searched to find my Bible, I would thank God for a live-in example and reminder of someone who was sharpening me spiritually (Prov. 27:17).

In some cases, your spiritual devotion may prompt your spouse to seek Jesus more intently, but in other situations, the distance between the two spiritual pursuits can widen over time. Many couples struggle with experiencing unity regarding their religious convictions. If your spouse lacks a commitment to the local church, a desire to obey the teachings of Scripture, or a longing to nurture a walk with Jesus, it puts you in an unfortunately compromising position. If one spouse shows spiritual vitality and the other shows spiritual apathy, the most central part of one's life is unaligned with the most important human relationship in one's life.

Your faith is different than any other component of your life. At least, it should be. If your faith doesn't alter everything else about you, I sincerely doubt it is biblical faith.

For a husband to support a wife's church involvement but unwilling to go himself is not the same as having various religious preferences. Having different personal interests is not the same as having different spiritual commitments. It's not a big deal if he likes action movies and she likes chick flicks. She can enjoy going out, and he prefers to stay home, and they can make that work. The Christian faith is not as easy to alienate from one another. Christianity is more than a system of beliefs to accept; it's a Savior to follow. Jesus is going places, and he commands his followers to come along (Mark 1:17; Luke 9:23-24). It doesn't work to have Jesus a part of your life – he is your life (Col. 3:4). If you want to follow Jesus and he turns right, what happens if your spouse turns left? The two of you end up in different places.

That's probably why the New Testament warns about marrying someone who isn't a believer. You become unequally yoked (2 Cor. 6:14). Imagine two oxen paired together for plowing but they each have their own direction to which they focus. It's not going to be a prosperous day in the field. It won't be for your marriage either. What do you do if you are married to an unbeliever? You stay married (1 Cor. 7:13). Use your godly commitment to your spouse (1 Pet. 3:1) to be used by God to bring him or her to saving faith (1 Cor. 7:16).

What do you do if you are married to a believer who possesses a different level of maturity than you? For some, a deep spirituality may have never been present, but for others, you may have watched a gradual decline that is immensely disturbing. Where he or she once had a sincere dedication to Jesus, you are worried now about an apparent lukewarm association with Jesus. Your best chance to address your spouse's apathy is your personal integrity.

I will walk with integrity of heart within my house (Ps. 101:2).

Don't walk with Jesus out of drudgery but out of delight. Let your spouse see more of your walk than your talk. In this psalm, David proclaims a commitment that his life will display the intentions of his heart for his family to see it. Too often, our churches see the spiritual side of us and our families see the spiteful side of us. Live in such a way that even if your family doesn't believe what you believe, they at least believe that you believe it.

Nagging might produce immediate results but not longterm changes. Your spouse may respond to guilt for a season, but you must long for desire over duty. You want your spouse to follow Jesus – not be forced to go to church.

Don't allow your spouse's spiritual apathy to dilute your personal devotion.

Whether you continue on this journey alone or together, here are some things to consider to fight against the cancer of spiritual apathy in our lives. Be diligent to devote time with your God, prioritize commitment to your church, and maintain intentionality with your spouse. As you walk with integrity of heart around your house, let your spouse see the difference that hearing and doing the Word makes in your life (James 1:22).

Prayerfully, he or she will connect all your time in the Word and on your knees to be the reason for the abundant vitality emanating out of our life. Commit to a local church and don't forsake assembling with these people – they will spur you on to love and good deeds even when you don't feel like it (Heb. 10:24-25). As you grow, be intentional to share with your spouse out of the overflow of your heart (Matt. 12:34) how you are developing.

Don't preach to your spouse on why Bible reading should be a priority for him or her, only joyfully share what you are learning. Let them see your example more than they hear your exhortation. The spiritual climate in your home won't change until someone adjusts the thermostat. Get started today.

What God has joined together, let no spiritual apathy separate.

29 - Let No Spiritual Apathy Separate

READ: Psalm 1:1-6

REFLECT: Would you be pleased if your spouse or your children imitated your spiritual devotion?

RESPOND: Are you where you want to be spiritually? Talk with your spouse where you are and where you hope to be.

30
Let No Pride Separate

Your marriage will never heal until you view your pride as part of the sickness.

Pride is poisoning your marriage. If the husband or the wife refuses to receive correction, heed advice, or acknowledge wrongdoing, the marriage suffers from constant disarray. You probably know how frustrating it can be to see someone else's faults while he or she refuses to admit them. Have you ever been so dumbfounded at how clearly you can see it and how blind your spouse seems to be to the issue at hand? If you do, then you and your spouse agree on more than you probably realize. Your spouse has most likely felt the same way about you.

Marriage can be fertile soil for pride or humility. It all depends on what you plant and what you water. The nature of marital oneness creates a particular ability to expose vanity like no other relationship. This environment can make you more humble or cause your pride to plant its feet more rooted in the dirt. This person who knows you in every possible intimate way has seen you at your best but also at your worst. While the particular handling of such experiences can prove to be helpful or hurtful, the reality is inescapable – you haven't consistently shown this person your best side at all moments. He or she knows you intimately, and that might scare you to death.

> **When pride comes, then comes disgrace,**
> **but with the humble is wisdom (Prov. 11:2).**

Your pride has led you to sin against God and to hurt your spouse. Your ego doesn't want to admit your wrongdoing because the potential of disgrace shouldn't be lumped on someone as put together as you think you are. Instead of humbly showing a wise perspective of admitting sin and seeking restoration, pride will cause you to double-down and to make the matters continuously worse.

As if your own pride wasn't destructive enough, your spouse struggles with the same catastrophic issue. If you and your spouse both pridefully wait for the other to retreat from a position and repent of an attitude, you might be waiting forever. The conflict will inevitably increase.

It makes sense why a father would write to his son that "it is better to live in a corner of the housetop than in a house shared with a quarrelsome wife" (Prov. 21:9). A quarreling house indicates that one or both spouses are operating without keeping pride in check. Every quarrel among us is due to our passions warring inside us – not outside of us (James 4:1). All these sinful thoughts, words, and actions originate from pride which God himself opposes (James 4:6).

It's always easier to spot pride in your spouse's life than it is to acknowledge it in your own life. My wife once communicated something that she needed from me. Her suggestion was a valid request, but I had some serious defensive reservations that day. As she asked for one simple thing, my mind went to all the countless things I thought I was doing well. My stellar skills as a husband should have given me a free pass by now and kept me from any more requests.

While I communicated my thoughts (and others I just processed in my mind), my desired comeback was to remind her of just how good she had it in being married to someone like me. In my "humble" opinion, I was way better than any other husband she might know, and so she should thank her lucky stars that she got to be married to someone as kind, compassionate, and hard-working as me.

My prideful defense of myself as a man caused me to be a lesser husband for her. The haughty spirit present in me refused to address my weaknesses because I wanted her to focus on my strengths. I couldn't become a better husband because I acted like there wasn't any room to improve.

The only solution for pride is humility. For the glory of God and the sake of your marriage, you must humbly acknowledge that you are at least some part of the problem. As you work through the devastation that pride leaves in its wake, here are some wise steps of humility to put into practice.

First, humbly acknowledge that your spouse's words might be right. I know it is hard to accept, but you could be wrong. You might not be completely wrong, but is there a chance that you might be a percent of the problem? Even if the conflict is layered with years of frustration and myriads of misunderstandings, there is most likely some truth to the hard thing he or she is saying about you. As far as it depends on you, live at peace (Rom. 12:18) with your spouse and acknowledge the potential of your divisive contributions.

Second, humbly acknowledge that your spouse's feelings might be justified. It is pointless and unthoughtful to argue your intentions against your spouse's feelings. Even if you didn't mean to make your spouse feel that way, you can't argue with someone's feelings. Explain your intentions but acknowledge his or her perspective. Don't cause greater frustrations by attempting to invalidate deep-seated convictions.

Finally, humbly acknowledge that your spouse's forgiveness might be needed. Admit your mistakes and recognize your responsibility regardless of what your spouse says or does. Do not wait for an explicit confession on his or her part before you offer your own. Decide that you will humbly seek forgiveness for the role of which you are responsible. Pride will make you want to be right. Humility will cause you to make it right.

Seek to win your spouse more than you seek to win the argument.

Your argumentative skills might earn you a victory in a debate, but they also might land you a defeat in your marriage. If you prove your point and win the conflict, is your marriage in a better place because of it? Pride will seek a win for you, but humility will seek a win for the marriage.

What God has joined together, let no pride separate.

30 - Let No Pride Separate

READ: Proverbs 16:18-19

REFLECT: How is pride affecting your marriage?

RESPOND: Listen to and address your spouse's concern regarding your contributions to the issues in your marriage. Would you humbly admit your fault in the relationship?

31
Let No Sin Separate

You cannot give your spouse a love that you have not received.

Jesus taught us that nothing should separate a marriage (Mark 10:9). Then how is it possible that we have just walked through thirty concepts that do a pretty good job at it? In reality, this book could continue to add quite a few extra culprits that seem to separate quite a few marriages.

As you read through the previous chapters, you might have seen areas in which you need to improve. Our perspective guarantees that you saw areas in which you hope your spouse addresses. Even if you are in a bad marriage, I have often said that there is never a completely one-sided divorce. Even if one party contributed 99% of the conflict, the other spouse hasn't been perfect.

While I have counseled that logic for years, I have changed my mind recently regarding that claim. After years of teaching, writing, and counseling, I did discover a dysfunctional marriage that was ultimately one party's fault. In this particular case, the wife had been adulterous, disrespectful, ungrateful, accusatory and unwilling to provide anything for the husband. On the other hand, the husband had been nothing less than sacrificial, patient, forgiving, and willing to do not only his part but even her part to make the marriage work. Every time she numerously betrayed the marriage vows, he sought her out time and time again. Her mistakes cost him more than they cost her. And yet, he pursued her passionately. I had never seen anything like it.

Do I sound like I am making this marriage up? I have good news to share with you – this marriage is the most real thing in the world. It is the love Jesus has for his bride – the people of God. Scripture illustrates that the Church is the beloved Bride of Christ (Rev. 21:2, 9; Isa. 54:5; John 3:29). A wedding will soon take place, and somehow this perfect groom will follow through and make it all the way down to the altar to marry the most unfaithful of brides who will somehow be clothed in radiant white (Rev. 19:7-9).

How could such an unfaithful bride be arrayed in such purity? It can't be because she brought those clothes herself. The Bride of Christ is made up of wretched sinners like me (Rom. 7:24)!

Here's how this good news plays out for us. We were created in God's image (Gen. 1:26-27) and were meant to bring him glory (Col. 1:16). We rebelled against him repeatedly (Rom. 3:23) causing our sins to separate us from him (Isa. 59:2). God demonstrated his love for us in that while we were still sinners, he sent Jesus to die for us (Rom. 5:8). After our consistent inconsistency, Christ went to the cross with joy (Heb. 12:2) because of his great love (Eph. 2:4), and he is eagerly anticipating his wedding day with a bride dressed in a white gown which he purchased with his red blood.

> *For all have sinned and fall short of the glory of God, and are justified by his grace as a gift, through the redemption that is in Christ Jesus (Rom. 3:23-24).*

We are all sinners. We don't deserve the love of our spouse, and we definitely don't deserve the love of our Lord. The only way we can go to the chapel for the wedding ceremony is because he made a way for us to get there. Just like Hosea repurchasing his prostitute of a wife, Jesus bought us with his blood. He had to buy something back that already belonged to him!

While we have fallen short of God's glory, we are justified as righteous before him all because of grace. It is the wedding gift he gives to us. Through the blood of Jesus, redemption is found in Christ Jesus as he bleaches our sin-stained garments.

Most likely, while this book might have taught you some tips to help your marriage, your sin was probably more exposed than relieved.

Even if you attempt to address all the concerns that this volume high-lighted, your valiant efforts will reveal how hopeless you are. You have broken and will continue to break the commandments in the Bible and fail to perfect the principles expressed in this book. The success of your marriage doesn't have to be contingent upon your perfection but on the perfection of Jesus. He kept his vows because we were unable to keep ours.

To receive the good news means that you believe Jesus took your pun-ishment so that you could obtain his salvation. By faith, would you receive his grace? Do you believe that you can experience complete forgiveness for all of your past, present, and future sins through the sacrifice Jesus made on the cross? Jesus was eager and willing to take God's punishment for your sins so you can experience God's power for your salvation.

Sin distorted the first marriage. Adam and Eve sinfully chose their way, and the rebellion's consequences devastated every marriage after that. But Scripture teaches that there is still a wedding day yet to come. While sin marred the first marriage, grace will transform the last one.

The only way for your marriage to work is if Jesus' love is the standard and the source. The only chance we can even comprehend or offer love is because he first loved us (1 John 4:19). Our marriages are intended to reflect this type of unending commitment to one another (Eph. 5:25-27).

While sin separates you from God and your spouse, the gospel can reconcile you to both.

How do you trudge through all the mistakes in your marriage? We forgive one another with the type of forgiveness by which we were forgiven (Col. 3:13). If Jesus doesn't see my forgiven spouse as con-demned (Rom. 8:1), how could I condemn her? If God remembers my wife's sins no more (Jer. 31:34), how could I bring them back up again? If he removed her transgressions as far as the east is from the west, they must be removed from my map as well. Your marriage needs the grace of Jesus. Good thing he is ready to offer it.

What God has joined together, let no sin separate.

31 - Let No Sin Separate

READ: Ephesians 2:1-10

REFLECT: How should the gospel change your marriage?

RESPOND: Have you received the gospel of grace for your salvation?
Will you offer that same type of grace to your spouse?

For more books, sermons, posts, articles, and resources, visit **travisagnew.org**.

34497305R00076

Made in the USA
Columbia, SC
15 November 2018